LOST

ALASKA

Printed in the United States of America

TABLE OF CONTENTS

ACKNOWLEDGEMENTS

I would like to thank the pastoral staff of Church on the Rock for the hard work, prayer and faith they put into this book to make it a reality, for the vision they had from the beginning and the effort they put into making this book come to life; and the people of Church on the Rock for their boldness and vulnerability in telling the stories that comprise this compilation of real-life stories.

This book would not have been published without the amazing efforts of our project manager, Diane Popenhagen. Her untiring resolve pushed this project forward and turned it into a stunning victory. Thank you for your great fortitude and diligence. I would also like to thank our invaluable proofreader, Melody Davis, for all the focus and energy she has put into perfecting our words. Lastly, I want to extend our gratitude to Ann Clayton, our graphic artist, whose talent and vision continually astounds us. We are so blessed to have you as a part of this team.

Daren Lindley
President and CEO
Good Catch Publishing

The book you are about to read
is a compilation of authentic life stories.
The facts are true, and the events are real.
These storytellers have dealt with crisis, tragedy, abuse
and neglect and have shared their most private moments,
mess-ups and hang-ups in order for others to learn and
grow from them. In order to protect the identities of those
involved in their pasts, the names and details of some
storytellers have been withheld or changed.

INTRODUCTION

You are about to step into the lives of six individuals who were imprisoned by bad choices or unfortunate circumstances and were spiraling into a dark vortex of hopelessness and despair.

When your life has become dominated by situations beyond your control, and you're plagued by emotions you don't know how to handle, you quickly find yourself scrambling for the reason for your existence in a world that has become so very dark.

Many have traveled this road full of broken promises, shattered dreams, abuse and painful memories. I invite you to read the following six accounts of those who have not only survived but are now thriving in a purpose-filled life that has been recovered and restored.

In the following pages you will discover that your failures do not remove your possibilities; your mistakes or what people have done to you do not remove your right to future fulfillment. You can change; you can be restored, and your dreams can be fully realized.

These are ordinary people who refused to give up and fought their way to freedom. They did not disqualify themselves or choose to live in the shadows of yesterday. Now they thrive with a sense of mission and purpose; may these stories inspire you to do the same.

ARRESTED BY GOD'S GRACE
THE STORY OF BRAD
WRITTEN BY JASON CHATRAW

I couldn't tell which was louder — the fists pounding on my door or my heart pounding in my chest. One preceded the other, but they both meant one thing: My reign as southern Illinois' meth king was over.

I suppose I should have been more scared about the consequences. Over the previous six months, I had committed enough crimes to send me away to prison for a lifetime. But when law enforcement officials busted through the door of my house on January 14, 2002, I didn't care. Relief better described my demeanor while officers handcuffed me and carted me away to jail.

I was done running — from the law.

પ્રભ

Wearing prison orange was never part of my life plan but a likely result given the hand dealt to me. My father was a committed Baptist. He worked incessantly to provide for our family and had our family in church every Sunday, whether we liked it or not. And we didn't. However, the story of God's grace and forgiveness briefly penetrated my heart when I was 8 years old and confronted with the reality of life and death after my cousin died in a four-wheeler accident. I quickly responded at church, repeating a salvation prayer. But no matter what Christian values my dad and the church tried to instill in me, I still couldn't escape the ill effects of living with my mom.

Church felt fake. We wore forced smiles and acted as if everything in our lives resembled an episode of *Leave it to Beaver*. Then we came home to the living nightmare that was my mom.

On Sundays after church, the fighting commenced in the car before we were even out of the church parking lot. My mom yelled and screamed at my dad. She screamed at us, too. But that was tame to the other exploits that consumed her time while my dad was busy working. On more than one occasion, I came home to discover my mom in the arms of another man, as she had multiple affairs. Drugs and alcohol became her true companions, "friends" she couldn't live without. And it's easy to see why.

My mom's childhood was challenging to say the least. She experienced her own nightmares, watching her mother kill herself with a .44 Magnum being chief among them. Self-medicating seemed inevitable for her, and she fully embraced it.

When I was 10 years old, my parents divorced. And my nightmare was only beginning. Despite my mom's battle with drugs and alcohol, she gained custody of me. Given more freedom with no accountability, my mom's drinking and drug habits grew exponentially. As a result, she became lax in her discipline of me. I could get away with so much more. And I did, taking full advantage of the new permissive environment in our home.

Largely ignored at home by my mom, I became a loud child, doing whatever I could to get people's attention. But over time, I realized that getting people's attention wasn't enough to satisfy the gaping hole in my heart. I needed to fill it with other things, anything to ease the pain of the situation I had been thrust into. By age 13, I found what I thought I was looking for with some friends who shared similar painful home lives, if you could even consider it "life." They introduced me to their coping mechanisms. Before I knew it, my weekends became a standing appointment with my fellow despondent friends and two other new pals: alcohol and pot.

But who would blame me? No child or teenager should have to deal with the horrors I experienced growing up. When my mom would run out of drugs, she would go on a rampage. Raging over the fact that she had nothing to snort, smoke or drink, my mom would remember with striking clarity all my recent misdeeds and punish me accordingly. She would cock her arm, clenching her fist, and stare at me with wild eyes. Then she would strike. *Whack!* The loving hands that cared for me as a baby were now coiled as a weapon. She hit me as hard as any guy had ever hit me. This wasn't the way any child was supposed to grow up.

❧❧❧

LOST

Watching my mom accelerate down a harmful path inspired me to begin searching for other alternatives. Despite my own dabbling with drugs and alcohol, I knew that I was slowly joining her on a destructive journey. There had to be another way to live. I found some satisfying answers at a local Pentecostal church my new girlfriend took me to with her parents. Instead of having a negative view of church, I returned with a different perspective, one that fully understood my need for grace and forgiveness. I started to feel hopeful about life again.

One Sunday at a large evening gathering, I listened to a pastor preach an amazing message about God's love and grace. When he finished, he invited everyone who wanted to begin following Christ to come forward and pray. I didn't hesitate. I had prayed a similar prayer when I was 8, but I understood more this time. This time, it seemed real — so much so that I got baptized *that* night.

The following week, I returned to the church to learn more. After the sermon, the pastor called me out by name.

"Brad, there's an anointing on your life to preach and evangelize," he pronounced from the stage.

He invited me to come forward so he and others could pray for me. I started running down the aisle. That night, I experienced the presence of God in a very powerful way. About 200 people from the church surrounded me and began praying over the direction of my life. As people began praying for me, I became weak and could no longer stand. Now, I was finally running in the right direction.

A week after I turned 16, I moved out of the house. My

mom grew increasingly upset over the fact that I started attending church and was getting my life together. Maybe I suddenly reminded her too much of my dad, but she wasn't happy about my new decision to follow Jesus. So she expressed herself, punching and beating me in the face. The next day, I was gone.

I dropped out of school to work two jobs to support myself and afford my new apartment. It wasn't ideal, but neither was getting punched around by my mother. However, I began to grow in my faith in unexpected ways.

All those predictions about how I was going to be an evangelist began to come true. Everywhere I went — whether it was to work or eat or hang out — I seemed to have an opportunity to talk about my faith. Amazingly, about 90 percent of the people I invited to church eventually came. I had no fear at all. My life was living proof that God could make a broken soul whole again. If I mustered up the courage to mention God, he would give me the words to say. No one would ever describe my way with words as eloquent, but when I shared my faith with others, it grabbed people's attention. God used me in powerful ways.

But I started running again.

ॐ ॐ ॐ

As I was growing in my faith, I was also developing a deep relationship with my girlfriend and her parents. Their influence in my life was immeasurable. Without their encouragement to pursue a relationship with God, I don't know if I could have survived that tenuous time after moving out of my mom's house. Amidst the shambles of my broken family, her parents became my surrogate parents. I had my own apartment, but I ate dinner with them almost every night of the week.

But then things began to unravel.

My girlfriend and I had a great relationship, and because of that, her parents were eager to see us tie the knot. They went so far as to give us a ring and urge me to propose to her. I was 18, and she was 16. While I was young, I had developed a good discipline of meditating on God's word and praying about many decisions in my life. As I prayed about this being the right time or not to propose, I felt like it just wasn't time yet. I wasn't ready. And that was the beginning of the end.

After I refused to comply with her parents' wishes, it didn't take long for my girlfriend to break up with me. It was a tough time for me. I had grown to love and trust her parents, but they had now forced us apart. There was a sudden void of spiritual leadership in my life. This loss of trust grew to cynicism — and I began to doubt. Instead of searching for answers in the Bible and through prayer, I sought other means to assuage my doubts. My connection with God seemed to wane in the midst of this breakup — and it didn't take long before it was all but gone.

Over the previous two years, the people who had become my friends were the people I was aggressively sharing my faith with — addicts and drunks. So when I turned to them for help, they offered me all they knew: drugs and alcohol.

"When an impure spirit comes out of a person, it goes through arid places seeking rest and does not find it. Then it says, 'I will return to the house I left.' When it arrives, it finds the house swept clean and put in order. Then it goes and takes seven other spirits more wicked than itself, and they go in and live there. And the final condition of that person is worse than the first." (Luke 11:24-26)

Once I began returning to a familiar pattern of self-medicating, the despondency and despair I was experiencing, the power of Satan over my life, seemed stronger than ever. When I started falling back into my old way of living, I fell hard. Almost immediately, I started doing cocaine and LSD. I even resorted to selling drugs to pay for my habit.

It wasn't long before I met a girl, too. Stacy was her name. She was sweet and paid attention to me — and that was all I needed at the time. She was also a fellow drug addict. We started living together, and before we knew it, she was pregnant with my oldest daughter, Heaven. Yet even having a child in the home wasn't enough to curtail my junky tendencies.

My nosedive off a cliff had barely started.

LOST

As I continued using drugs, I would try anything I could get my hands on. For the most part, I worked hard to maintain my habit. I didn't steal for money to buy my drugs. I earned it — or sold some drugs on the side. I maintained a busy lifestyle.

When my daughter was 14 months old, I ran into an old friend of mine from high school. He came over to my house and brought a new drug that I had never tried before. He called it meth.

I had heard of meth before but had never tried any. It took all of two seconds for me to snort it up my nose — and wow! The feeling it gave me was amazing. Meth gave me a tremendous high in a matter of seconds — and it kept me high for a long time. It didn't take long before I was hooked.

For the next four months, I started using meth off and on, more on than off. Its addictive powers are nearly impossible to break with sheer willpower alone. And away I went. I fell in love with meth. I couldn't get enough. For me, it was the nearly flawless drug, except for those vicious hours coming down off of it.

But its effect on my life was visibly destructive. It made me crazy. My behavior became erratic. When I started to come down, I never knew what I would do. My ears popped, creating excruciating pain. It pushed me to the brink of insanity. One night when I started coming down off a meth high, I grabbed my shotgun and put a slug in it. The gun was cold in my sweaty hands. I wondered if I had the nerve to pull the trigger as I put the gun to my head.

Not only did I have to resist my own urges to end it all — I also had to overcome Stacy.

Stacy, also strung out on meth, shifted her weight nervously, tempting me to end the tension. "Do it! I dare you!" she yelled.

I don't know what stopped me, but I decided to put the gun away. I awoke to a sobering reality: I was a danger to myself when coming down off meth.

Instead of using that moment of enlightenment to motivate me to leave my drug addiction behind, I used it as a motivator to go deeper into the world of drugs. I would now become a meth chef.

ॐॐॐ

Arriving at the conclusion that coming down off meth was my problem, having an endless supply of meth was my solution. If I never had to crash, all would be well. I could make all I wanted.

After asking around, I learned about different ways to cook meth, even though I had never actually seen someone make it. But I thought I could figure it out on my own. It seemed like a relatively simple, though involved, process. So I gathered all the ingredients and headed out into the woods to see if I could make it myself. Cooking meth in the great outdoors helped me avoid having the odor of burnt plastic emanating from my body. I figured it was best to let those things dissipate into the wild.

That night in the southern Illinois woods, I learned

there were a few things I was pretty good at. Making meth was at the top of the list.

I pocketed some of the finished sample to share with a few close friends to get their opinion. The feedback was unanimous: My meth was the best they ever had, and I should make more. Instantly, people said uplifting things about me and my meth. There were people coming from all over to get it, even as far away as Canada. People were lining up to help me make and distribute it. I quickly doubled the price and ramped up my manufacturing capabilities. I had a bona fide operation, complete with employees on a payroll and strategic distribution sites.

No longer was I just a drug addict — now I was an unsuspecting drug kingpin.

❧ ❧ ❧

I never wanted to be a drug dealer. It just kind of happened, mostly as a result of my skillful cooking and the sheer joy I experienced over making meth. But the amount of secrecy, treachery and deception that goes along with being a drug dealer kept me on edge. Avoiding the law was a rush for me at first; it was necessary in the midst of evil. But it didn't stay that way.

When my meth supply ran low, I disappeared into the woods to begin creating another batch. The immediate satisfaction I had over making meth was met with the irresistible urge to ensure that it was indeed top-shelf quality. I would break off enough for me and away I went.

I would stay up for days at a time, sometimes never leaving the woods as I survived on squirrels I shot and creek water — if I ate anything at all.

That's when the visions started, the kind that were more than nonsensical hallucinations. I even saw them sober. Demon spirits. Oftentimes, I would see a team of them, appearing in human form and surrounding me. They would watch me, talking to me and coaching me. On some nights, they would be acting so crazy that I would chase them away from me. These demonic spirits tormented me. In the woods or in my house, they followed me everywhere. Once I was drug free for two weeks and came home to see one of these spirits just sitting in the corner, watching me.

I wanted it all to stop — I just didn't know how. The drugs, the demons, the destructive forces at work in my life. It was driving me to the brink. Though I was being careful, it didn't take long before I began wishing DEA agents would catch up with me.

It wasn't long before my wish came true.

෧෧෧

On January 14, 2002, six months after my meteoric rise to the top, a couple of missteps toppled my reign as southern Illinois' meth king. The night before, Stacy and I got a babysitter for our daughter, Heaven, and ventured out into the woods to make another batch. I didn't like keeping all the instruments necessary to make drugs in the house, preferring to keep them in the woods to minimize the damage in case law enforcement officers caught me. We had just enough ingredients to make about a quarter pound of manufactured meth. After we mixed the chemicals, we let the smell die down and returned home with a liquefied batch that we decided to harden the following day.

On the morning of the 14th, I began the process of turning the liquid meth into the final version that would go on the street. I told Stacy to go get a guy I hadn't seen in a while and tell him to come over and try some. Later that day when he dropped by, he was wearing a wire — and I was done.

He left, and 30 minutes later officers began pounding on the door; Stacy opened the door to an onslaught of agents eager to apprehend me. I was sitting at the kitchen table surrounded by about eight pounds of meth in its liquid form. There was nothing I could do but surrender.

Officers handcuffed me, doped and ragged, and dragged my frail frame out of the house and into a squad car. What began as a hobby and a new way to satisfy my drug habit ended in felony charges.

Though it was easily the worst day of my life, I felt some relief. I knew I was going to die if I continued doing what I was doing. Being high on meth, up for 15 days at a time with no sleep and no meals — it was no way to live. I was barely alive to begin with.

Fortunately, I didn't have to run anymore.

ARRESTED BY GOD'S GRACE

❧❧❧

Long before agents came barreling through my house that day, God was already at work. Though it appeared that I had squandered everything God had given me, I was a captive audience to the power of God's love and grace in my life — I simply watched it unfold.

I immediately went to county jail and awaited my trial. I took a plea bargain and pled guilty. It took four court appearances before I could plead out. It was a difficult time for me. I was faced with a sentence of 25 years to life. Prosecutors talked tough. They were going to make an example out of me, they said. I had no idea if that was a scare tactic, but my court-appointed attorney told me it wasn't something the judge said very often. Adding to my angst was the fact that I had nobody to tell on. When you're the biggest fish in the pond, it leaves you with no options and nothing but a long fall. In just six months' time, I had become a notorious drug dealer, according to DEA officials. At the time, nobody was manufacturing more drugs than me in our area. Despair doesn't begin to describe how I felt about my situation.

However, things rapidly changed when the nearly eight pounds of liquid meth — the all-important evidence — discovered in my kitchen when they arrested me shrank to six grams when officials transferred it 45 miles from my home to Springfield, Illinois. Consequently, my minimum sentence of 25 years shrank to a maximum of six and a half years.

LOST

Then my uncle came to visit me.

At 6 feet, 7 inches tall, my uncle always looks like he means what he says, even if he doesn't. He came to visit me one day in jail.

"Do you remember what God promised you, Brad? You have new hope and a new life."

I nodded, recalling all those prophetic words, which seemed like a distant memory at this point. I said nothing.

"You're to read this Bible because you have the time to do it. Read it every day."

He handed me a Thompson's Chain Reference Bible. It wasn't a suggestion. But why not? I wasn't going anywhere for quite some time.

I was prepared to return to God's word, but I still wanted to get out of jail quickly. I told my dad where I hid my money and told him to go out and hire a lawyer to help me get out of this impending sentence. Though clearly miffed at the way I treated life so flippantly, my dad obliged. My dad hired a family lawyer who told him he could get me out of the sentence altogether with time served.

My dad didn't favor this idea at all, nor did he like the fact that I was going to get a brief furlough before returning to serve my time. I planned to spend one final night on a drug-induced binge before going to prison. My dad won.

I started to hear rumblings that I could get out with just 15 days served. This was working out better than expected. But being led by the Holy Spirit, my dad didn't want any such thing to happen. He wanted me to stay in prison and spend some time reflecting on God's goodness and grace as I read the Bible daily.

As I stayed in county jail awaiting my sentencing, I began reading the Bible. I started in Genesis and grabbed my pencil and took notes on what I read. I underlined stuff that I read and studied it some more. In just three and a half months, I read from Genesis to Revelation. I laughed. I cried. There were parts that so resonated with me that I read them all over again. I loved it. Reading the Bible was enjoyable. It was quiet, peaceful — all with three square meals a day. Based on where I came from, I couldn't beat it. I had my opportunity to get close to God, and I did it. I read it all the way through.

I had almost finished reading the Bible all the way through for the first time when my final appearance in court arrived. I was still holding out hope that I could get out of jail with time served. Then my lawyer delivered the shocking news, orchestrated by my cunning dad.

"Brad, you're going to do 12 months in prison, and you're going to a drug rehab program — and I'm taking your furlough away from you. You're not even getting out," my lawyer explained.

I said nothing, a silent protester. I failed to see the reasoning behind taking away my furlough. But God knew — and so did my dad. And away I went to state prison.

かかか

LOST

Once I moved to the prison system, I took the opportunity to delve into God's word. Unfortunately, I also got into some fights, as well.

I refused to join a gang, even though members from the various gangs were roughing me up. With no drugs and a healthy appetite, I began working out and filled out my 6-foot, 3-inch frame in a hurry. No longer skin and bones, I fought back when necessary, merely as a means of survival. But I wasn't just focused on my physical well-being. Suddenly, my spiritual well-being was at the forefront of my mind every day as I read the Bible.

Again and again, I read through the Bible. Then on April 14, 2003, one year to the day after I entered prison, I walked out of it a free man.

But I wasn't completely free yet.

ॐॐॐ

Once prison officials released me, I returned to my dad's house and had to be re-raised.

From eating at the dinner table — no elbows at the table, no smacking your mouth with food in it — to polite gestures when meeting a new acquaintance; I was a mess. The drugs garbled my sensibility, and I had become fairly unpredictable. My dad had to be a daddy to a little boy all over again. He did a good enough job that a few months later I managed to get a job working as a service provider for the local power plant where my dad worked.

In less than a year from my hire date, I rose from the

lowest position to plant manager after my manager hurt his back and couldn't work. I went from a $20,000 a year job to a $60,000 a year job. But with all this added pay came added responsibility. Instead of turning to the Bible, I returned to the bottle — and Stacy.

When I first got out of prison, I was doing well spiritually. I started attending church again, returning to the same mellow church I went to as a child with my parents. It was predictable and safe; it's what I needed. I even started working with the youth after helping lead a Vacation Bible School. God was changing my heart. This all came as a shock to Stacy.

When we got back together, the former destructive elements of my life were gone. I was doing well and headed down the right path. But Stacy wasn't. Before I knew it, I began sliding back into a few gripping vices.

For starters, Stacy wasn't the best relationship choice for me as I struggled to leave all my past behind. She had quit using meth, but she still snorted cocaine and smoked pot. And despite my best efforts to live right, I began living with Stacy.

Within a couple of months after getting back together, we got married, then Stacy got pregnant again. Things never got as crazy as they were before I went to prison, but all my vows to live a more pleasing life before God seemed hollow.

I knew my weaknesses, yet I chose to put myself in an environment that wasn't conducive to spiritual growth. I finally came to terms with what I knew to be true: My

LOST

relationship with Stacy was holding me back from my full potential in every aspect of my life.

Faced with another suffocating circumstance, I again didn't know what to do. Making good choices became difficult as my desires overrode Godly decision-making.

෬෬෬

I first noticed Rachel when she came to our plant to give her dad his lunch. It was almost a daily ritual. She had an easy way about her as she talked with her dad, who just so happened to work for me. I began to take notice of her with an unhealthy fondness. I was married to a drug addict. Rachel was the antithesis of Stacy — and I wanted to get to know her more. It was an innocent enough crush at first, stealing glances at her from across the room. But with the right — or wrong — circumstances, it eventually blossomed into something more.

Rachel's beauty was what first arrested me, but I was also taken aback with the way her parents treated each other. Still together after 30 years — that made a deep impression on me. They loved each other, and they loved the Lord. I immediately realized Rachel was cut from the same cloth. *I want a woman like that!* I thought. As unhealthy and wrong as it was, she became the object of my affection.

Unbeknownst to me, Rachel also held an unhealthy infatuation with me. I had only spoken with her when she came to visit her father during lunch, until one day I ran into her at a local gas station. We were both pumping gas side by side and struck up a conversation. Just as she was leaving, she gave me her number.

It didn't take long before texting developed into coffee dates. We would simply meet and talk. It was nice to have someone who listened to me for a change. I knew it was wrong, but I was craving the intimacy of our conversations. I had never even had a guy friend who was close enough that I felt comfortable confiding in. I listened to her. She listened to me. It was only a matter of time before things became much more intimate than simply conversations.

About six months after Stacy gave birth to my son, Andrew, I got Rachel pregnant. Instead of remaining faithful to God and my wife, I complicated my life again.

When Rachel first told me she was pregnant, I became distraught. I thought Stacy would go crazy and divorce me because that's what usually happens. I knew it would be tough, but I thought it would probably be for the best, anyway. Stacy was upset and angry — but she wanted to stick with me, and I didn't want to divorce her just yet and watch my healthy income dwindle due to alimony payments. I researched the state's divorce laws and knew Illinois wouldn't be very favorable toward me if I ended up in court. I needed to move somewhere that was more sympathetic toward husbands and dads.

LOST

Even before I got Rachel pregnant, I began mulling over a move to Alaska. There were some career opportunities for me that were exciting and dangerous — and paid handsomely. Even more importantly, after some research, I concluded that the divorce laws in Alaska expressed sympathy for fathers and husbands. I wasn't exactly living for the Lord, so I had no problem scheming to keep more of my fat paycheck.

After I got the news about Rachel, I decided this was a good time to move. I asked Stacy to come with me along with the kids. She lasted three months before returning to Illinois. Unfortunately, she took Heaven and Andrew with her, leaving me alone and without my children. It was depressing.

I really wanted Rachel to come with me, but I knew it wasn't right — even though I was doing everything else wrong. What I feared most was losing my kids. Subjecting them to a drug-infested environment wasn't the best situation for raising them. So I began saving my money, determined to use every last penny, if that's what it took, to get my children back.

In August 2007, Rachel gave birth to our son, Caden. Now I had another child who was thousands of miles away — and he was with the woman I loved. Many lonely nights followed that fall in Alaska until I could return to work and not live with the ever-present reminder of my loneliness and pain. Once I returned from six months of work in April, I couldn't bear the loneliness anymore. I asked Rachel to join me in Alaska. She agreed with the one caveat that I divorce Stacy. I did — and promptly married Rachel in July 2008.

While I should have been happy, I still felt empty inside. I had traded my addiction to drugs and alcohol for an addiction to love and acceptance. Those things aren't bad on their own, but the way I arrived at them wasn't healthy. It was sinful — and just because I was now married to a woman devoid of a drug problem didn't mean everything was suddenly going to change.

But it did — and not for the better.

வேவேவே

Simply being sober was enough of a drastic difference for me that I thought Rachel was the perfect wife. If you are married long enough to someone who is burned out on drugs, you forget what *normal* is. But *normal* in our new home was short-lived when Stacy went to jail on a DUI charge. Stacy's legal troubles were enough to help me win my protracted custody battle. Almost overnight, Rachel went from being a mom to a 1-year-old son to a mom of three kids. This transition wasn't easy.

A few months later, I took a seasonal job on the North Slope, operating heavy equipment for an oil company. I left Rachel to care for the kids and got to work. The stress of my job, along with the fact that I wasn't there for my family, started to get to me. In the off-chance that I got a weekend off and was allowed to return home, I drank from the minute I walked in the door to the minute I left.

LOST

When my job finally ended, I came home and continued drinking heavily. I had been out of prison for quite some time, but I felt like I was still there.

What happened to all that freedom I experienced when I spent time reading the Bible and praying? Why was my life in shambles, despite my best efforts to make it look respectable?

My relationship with God was becoming a distant memory — but he hadn't given up on me.

❧❧❧

In the spring of 2009, I began my summer job, one that allowed me to come home every day and be with my family — and my alcohol. I began a routine of drinking a fifth of Jack Daniels every night after work along with a case of beer. Instead of coping with stress by turning to Christ, I found plenty of ways to self-medicate the pain.

My custody agreement with the court stated that my two kids with Stacy — Heaven and Andrew — would return to Illinois every summer to spend it with their mom. The Saturday night before we were preparing to fly the kids back to Illinois for the summer, I was drunk and having fun with them. I was driving up and down our long driveway in the mountains. No one was on the road, but I should have never been behind the wheel.

Just as we were about to put the kids down for the night, I decided I wanted to take them on one more drive. Rachel, realizing I was way too drunk to drive, rejected the idea — and it infuriated me. Without thinking, I backhanded her. I didn't knock her out. I didn't even leave a mark — but there was a mark on my soul, and my heart was hurting.

I got up early the next morning to drive to town to get some milk to make breakfast. I couldn't stop thinking about what I had done to Rachel. Here was a woman I loved so much, yet I had hurt her in an unthinkable way. I didn't want our marriage to start off in the wrong direction. But less than a year into our marriage, it was headed south quickly.

As I was driving down a main stretch of road in town, I noticed a little sign near an elementary school:

Church on the Rock
Palmer Campus
11:15 a.m.

I had never seen this sign before, but something was drawing me toward it. On my way back out of town, I decided to pull into the parking lot and have a look around.

"Can I help you?" asked a rough-looking man with crazy hair.

"I'm just checking this place out to see what it's about."

"You ought to come check it out some time," he replied. "Go in there. There are people to talk to."

It was exactly what I needed. It felt like the Holy Spirit was saying, "It's time to talk."

LOST

However, I didn't go inside. I went home but remained really excited about the church.

I told Rachel about it and expressed my intentions of attending it the following week upon our return from Illinois. The whole week we were in Illinois, I did nothing but drink. All the feelings of endearment from Rachel's parents were gone. Her dad disapproved of me, especially since his daughter was unhappy and far away from home. But her parents were praying, asking God to do something to transform us.

That next Sunday, the real transformation process began. I was a wreck from too much drinking on our trip, but I was determined to attend the Church on the Rock with my family — and Rachel, Caden and I did.

From the moment we stepped in the door of the church, the people were warm and inviting. The sermon deeply impacted me. We were hooked. Rachel fell in love with the church and the people there. It was evident that people at Church on the Rock loved God and loved others. The following Sunday, we rededicated our lives to God.

かかか

Since that time, God has been at work in my life in powerful ways. He restored my marriage (and Rachel and I shed plenty of tears on the phone asking Stacy to forgive us for what we did).

He began healing old wounds. He began teaching me how to live — again. Within a couple of months, I quit drinking alcohol of any kind. God began putting together the pieces of my broken life.

As this spiritual rehabilitation process began — I had to learn to re-walk spiritually — God began to wake me up in the middle of the night with dreams of preaching specific messages for specific churches. God also gave me visions of my children doing ministry when they were adults. Then I met with one of our pastors one day, and in the middle of our conversation, I remembered all the prophecies in my life spoken over me at 16 years old. And, man, it hit me like a ton of bricks what God has in store for me.

Church on the Rock has opened up opportunities for me to do different things — whether it's sharing my faith in a remote outpost in Nepal or doing mission work in Peru. I told one of our pastors what God spoke into my life years ago. He's helping me develop my leadership skills and this thing that God has in store for me. God is leading me.

One of my fears is public speaking, especially in an environment where I'm sitting down. I'm nervous about getting in front of people to speak, and my pastor knows that. But he said, "I want you to start praying for the kids in front of church." And he's slowly getting me up in front of the church to speak and to pray, and God's really doing that.

People have come up to us saying God is moving really fast in your life for a reason — it's like there is no time. Six months later, God has totally transformed our marriage.

LOST

Now I know what it means to be united with one in my life. When Rachel first moved to Alaska, we weren't living for the Lord. Now we are pursuing God together and have common purpose and vision. My wife is even totally accepting of my children, as if they were her own. That's what God has done for her. He has filled her with a new vision and purpose in life. He has done it for me, as well.

No longer do I have a reason to run. God has arrested me — and he has given me a heart for him.

IMPOSSIBLE ODDS – HAPPY ENDINGS
THE STORY OF CAROLINE
WRITTEN BY CONNIE RUTH CHRISTIANSEN

"Angie, look! It's Daddy!" My heart beat happily at the sight of him — *Daddy! Oh, how I've missed you.* Angie and I rushed across the schoolyard toward the familiar old pickup truck where Daddy was waiting. Throwing myself into his arms, I reveled in the familiar feel of those big strong arms. Daddy piled me into the pickup cab and then assisted Angie in climbing up next to me. He hopped in and stepped on the gas — the tires squealed as he sped out of the parking lot. "Wheeeee!" I giggled. "Go fast, Daddy, go fast." I gazed up expectantly at his face, waiting for a wink and a grin. But Daddy wasn't smiling. "Where are we going, Daddy?" My question was met with silence. I looked over at Angie. She put her finger to her lips and mouthed a silent "shhh." Since she was 9 — two years older than me — I considered Angie to be much wiser than I about life, so I obeyed her command to be quiet. I sat awkwardly between them wondering, *What's happening? What's wrong?* I leaned back against Daddy and watched the green signs on the freeway fly by. Daddy finally broke the silence by telling us about our new home. We drove for days talking about how great life in Canada was going to be; north through California, across Oregon and into Washington.

LOST

I lifted my sleepy head as the truck merged off the freeway. Daddy maneuvered the pickup through a residential neighborhood and rolled to a stop in front of a tall Victorian apartment. He leaned over and took a gun out of the glove box, commanding us to "Stay put!" while he went into Uncle's house to exchange the gun for money. I crawled over to the driver's seat window and peered out, waiting anxiously for Daddy to return. But what I saw were big black cars parking in the middle of the street and scary men with guns getting out. I clung to Angie in fear, when suddenly the driver's door flew open. Two men in black coats grabbed me; Angie screamed, "Caroline!" and began to yell and kick, fighting for her life as they grabbed her, too. I momentarily panicked, until out of the corner of my eye I noticed a police car door opening; Mama and Grandma were sitting in the back seat. And I somehow understood: *These men aren't here to hurt us. They're here to rescue us.*

ॐ ॐ ॐ

Daddy was my hero; I wanted to be just like him. He was warm and affectionate and made me feel special. At night, he would often crawl into bed with me — he was gentle and kind, and the things he did to me felt good. Mama, on the other hand, always seemed cold, distant; she was not affectionate at all. I didn't understand why Mama was so angry at me when she discovered Daddy naked in my bed, or why she told me to "never tell anyone," or why she wanted to keep me away from Daddy. Sometimes he was mean to her, but he was never mean to me.

Mama and Daddy were active in our community; they helped at the boy's orphanage and at our Baptist church. I enjoyed going to church with my family and Grandma; Mama was nice to me at church in front of people. I loved the music and hearing about Jesus. At 5 years old, I accepted Jesus as my Savior, and I was baptized in water. When Daddy lost his job, everything changed; he started gambling and drinking. We quit going to church; Mama had to work long hours to pay the bills. Craig, our second cousin, came to live with us. Craig was nice to me, and it wasn't long before he was taking Daddy's place. I was glad — I missed Daddy's affection, and Craig made me feel special, too. Craig was 15, and I was 4; I was head-over-heels in love.

అ అ అ

School was out for the weekend, and I was happy to be home. "I'm home," I hollered as I entered the front door. There was no answer. "Craig, I'm home!" Everything was dark and strangely quiet as I moved from room to room looking for signs of life — the rooms were empty. *That's strange. Craig is always here waiting for me to play house.* I climbed on the living room sofa, peered out the window and waited. But Craig never came home.

"Where's Craig?" I asked when Mama came home from work.

LOST

"He won't be living here anymore," she answered, without looking at me. "He's been drafted into the Army and is on his way to Vietnam. He'll be gone a very long time." Her words were like ice water. *He didn't even say goodbye!* I was devastated. No more Craig; Mama didn't love me. Daddy was gone most nights; when he was home, he was drunk, and Mama was always mad at him. I missed the way he used to be — I was afraid to be near him for fear that Mama would get mad at me.

❧❧❧

"Wake up! Hurry!" Mama was leaning over my bed, shaking me out of a deep slumber. "Hurry! Stuff whatever you want to take with you into this as fast as you can. Hurry!" She handed me a pillow case and woke Angie. We stumbled through the house, grabbing clothes and our favorite toys. *What's happening?* Mama hustled us out the door, into the car and drove away, away from Daddy. Mama always stood up to Daddy, even when he hit her. She protected us from him. I became scared of him, yet it was very confusing because I loved him so much.

❧❧❧

After the FBI picked Daddy up for kidnapping us from school, Mama sent us to live in foster care for a while. I lived with a family who had a son named Arnold. He was 14, and I was 8. One day, Arnold and his gang lured me into a garage, and one by one they sexually assaulted me. I was terrified — I struggled with all of my might to fight their sweaty, smelly bodies off of me, but to no avail. They left me lying in a crumpled heap, battered and very confused. It was the first time that sex had been physically painful. And it was the first time I realized that perhaps what my daddy had done to me was not a good thing. *Is that why Mama was angry? Did she think Daddy was hurting me? Is that why Mama sent Craig to Vietnam?*

Arnold and his gang taught me many things. I learned to smoke cigarettes, to burglarize businesses, to lie effectively and to live by my wits — skills that would prove most valuable in my later years. I didn't tell anyone about the gang rape. I was subdued by fear, afraid that Arnold would tell everyone about my gang activities. The secret I carried inside began to fester until I was consumed with rage. I was livid with Arnold and with my mother for abandoning me. Bent on revenge, I kept my eyes and ears open for an opportunity to make Arnold pay.

かかか

"Your mom says it's time to go home!" I called across the department store to Arnold — I was afraid to be alone with him.

"You can't tell me what to do! You get out of here, or I'll get you like the last time!" Arnold yelled back. He took a menacing step toward me; I turned and ran. My heart was pounding with fear, my thoughts were jumbled. *Where is the up escalator?!* I couldn't find it, so I jumped

LOST

onto a staircase moving downward and tried to climb against the movement. But my little legs were not fast enough. My sandal slipped off my foot, and I fell. Searing hot pain shot through my leg as metal ripped through my flesh. I somehow managed to pull myself up and climb to solid ground. I never told Mama that night when she came to pick me up for my weekend visit.

I awoke from my sleep, crying out, "Mama!" Blood was pouring from my nose, and my body felt as if it were on fire. Grandma threw me into a cold bath, and Mama called the doctor. By the time I was rushed to Children's Hospital, my temperature was 107; I was in sepsis shock. I was quarantined in ICU, but a thorough examination proved that I was not contagious, that the cut on my leg was the reason for my infection.

"What happened to your leg?" the doctor asked.

"Arnold pushed me down the escalator," I lied. That lie triggered a police investigation.

"Please tell the truth, Caroline!" Mama pleaded with me. "Arnold says he didn't push you." I felt a sense of pleasure in having this power over him, knowing he was frightened. The social workers and police officers questioned me over and over. They kept reminding me of the consequences of my accusations — that since Arnold already had a criminal record, this incident would send him away for a very long time. My 8-year-old conscience raced with thoughts of revenge and guilt mixed with prayers and self-justification. *God, I know I should tell the truth, but Arnold deserves to be punished for raping me!*

Besides, it will do him good to be in reform school. He might come out a better person. I swallowed my guilt, stuck to my story and waited with satisfaction until Arnold was convicted and sentenced.

கௐௐ

My leg healed, and I was released from the hospital. Mama and Angie were already living with my new stepdaddy, and I joined them. *I am a stranger here; I don't even know this man.* We were continually moving in order to stay one step ahead of Daddy. In spite of a restraining order, he threatened to find us, to hurt Mama and to take us girls again. At every new school, I was getting into fights, failing class, stealing, lying and looking for love with every boy I met. Mama and Stepdaddy sent me to the best counselors and tutors, but nothing they did for me quieted my anger, eased my pain or filled my loneliness.

I could never tell Angie or anyone my secrets. Angie excelled at everything, but nothing I did pleased Mama, and Stepdaddy showed his disdain by beating me. When I was 13, Daddy was sent to prison for murder, and for the first time in six years, we stopped running. My daddy and Craig's affection was all I knew; I still confused that with love. I longed for love deep inside my heart, and I soon found drugs and alcohol to numb my feelings.

When I was 16, Angie graduated from high school and headed off for college. I thought that by having Mama to myself I could change the way she felt about me — I could make her love me. But Mama wanted to send me away, so with no reason to stay, I left home. I ended up on the streets, and there I did whatever it took to survive. I lived under bridges and in abandoned buildings. I committed crimes and sold my body for money. But I never begged — I was too proud. I'd rather die than beg for help! Continually on the move, my thumb and I hitchhiked from one state to the next, trying to find a place to call home and someone to love me. Car after car, man after man, I traveled, and I searched.

ฅฅฅ

"Hop in. Where are you headed?" He was just another man in a car, just another ride to somewhere.

"Nowhere, just take me as far as you can." I pulled my long legs into his tiny Volkswagen bug.

"Wanna come home with me — hang out a while, maybe get high?"

I had no money, food or shelter, no plans, so I answered with a casual, "Sure, why not?"

Ted was a tall intimidating figure: about 6 feet, 5 inches, unshaven face, shifty eyes, rumpled clothes. His home was cold and dark; it smelled musty, as if the doors and windows were rarely opened to air it out. As we walked through the house, I noticed locks and deadbolts on several bedroom doors. *Wow, this guy is really paranoid.* As if in answer to my thoughts, Ted broke the silence by explaining, "I have roommates — we use locks to protect our stuff." He led me to his bedroom; the only furniture in the room was a large bed and an antique wooden chest. He opened the chest to show me his very extensive stamp collection. *A stamp collection? This guy is so weird!* There was a bathroom directly off the bedroom, and there Ted filled two syringes, one for me and one for him, with a mixture of heroin and crystal meth. I had never used heroin before, and the extreme high took me by surprise. I liked the high, but it scared me. I had never felt anything that powerful.

I woke up the next morning in Ted's bed — he was gone. I walked to the door and pulled on the handle — the door was locked. "Hey! Let me out!" I hollered and banged on the door, but no one answered. I tried the windows, but they were nailed shut, and there was no way out. Panic set in as I realized, *I'm a prisoner; he's not going to let me out of here.* For the next few months, Ted kept me locked up most of the time, forcing me to take drugs and have sex with him. At first, I tried to fight back, but it was no use. I started experiencing hallucinations and hearing voices in my head, and the drugs became a welcomed escape. Eventually, it was easier to believe that I was his girlfriend and that I somehow belonged in the strange world he had arranged for me.

On occasion, Ted would let me out of the room and even take me on outings from the house, but I wasn't allowed to talk with anyone. After a time, I was completely brainwashed; he could leave me alone in the car, keys in the ignition, and I wouldn't even try to run. My very existence was dependent upon Ted's wishes. So when he was uncharacteristically missing for several days, I was worried. Locked away from food and with no drugs to feed my habit, I became violently ill. I prayed for my kidnapper to return home. It never occurred to me that someone else would come.

Ted's roommates were all drug addicts. They knew he held me captive. One of them was a woman who had been waiting for a chance to rescue me. After Ted had been missing for several days, she busted the door down. She found me in such bad shape, the first thing she did was give me dope to stop the withdrawals. I looked up from putting the needle in my arm and was surprised to see my sister standing in the doorway. *Angie! Oh, my God, what are you doing here? How did you find me? You shouldn't be here; this place is dangerous.* Ted's roommate had brought her along.

"Let's go home, Caroline." Angie tried to coax me out of the room.

"I can't go." I wanted to go, but I was terrified that Ted would find me and hurt Angie. I wasn't making any sense to Angie; she finally gave up and left me. *Angie, don't leave me!* I sat on the bed, the door to my prison busted open, but fear paralyzed me. Later that night, one of Ted's friends, Charlie, came by to take me "somewhere safe." He said Ted was in jail — I went willingly. Charlie took me to his home, a third-story apartment downtown. Both he and his wife, Nina, were drug addicts, but they were compassionate people and had no tolerance for Ted's treatment of me. They gave me a place to stay, and I knew kindness for a while, until the cops came. They busted Charlie and Nina. I was alone again. *I need to get out of here?* I was so confused; I didn't know where to go, and I didn't know how to find Angie. I didn't want to go back on the streets, so I stayed in the abandoned apartment hoping that Nina would come back.

Ted got out of jail and came to find me at Charlie's place. I needed a fix bad! What I didn't know was that Ted had mixed a lethal dose for me: a combination of crystal meth, cocaine, heroin, PCP and LSD. When it hit my bloodstream, I knew something was wrong — I feared I was going to die. He forced me onto the bed and raped me. And then, somehow I found the will to fight back. I began to struggle. "It's no use," he snarled. "The drugs I gave you are going to kill you, anyway. Why fight it?" He began throwing me around the room like a ragdoll. I kicked him hard and ran out onto the balcony. *If I can just jump from the balcony to that tree, I can climb to safety and find help.* Ted grabbed for me, and I jumped — I missed the tree and fell three stories to the sidewalk. Upon impact, I could feel my back breaking, then the drugs took over; my body collapsed, and my spirit left me. I watched from above as the ambulance arrived. The paramedics pronounced me dead, pulled a sheet over my head and waited for the police to arrive.

❧❧❧

LOST

I saw my life flash before my eyes as I was waiting in the darkness. I wasn't in heaven; I wasn't in hell — I was somewhere in between. "Jesus!" I cried out. "Help me!" And there he was, coming from the great light. He stood at a distance, but I could see every detail in his face and hear every word he was saying. Behind him was an incredible bright light; it was coming from a place that I couldn't see, but it was so enormous that nothing could contain it. Jesus stood before it, shielding me from it. I'd never known such love like I did at that moment. "Let me go back; give me a chance to love you while I'm still on earth," I implored. He explained to me that it would not be an easy journey, then he opened the heavens and revealed to me the torment and agony below. "I want to try. I want to tell others about your love and that you are real." Then I asked Jesus, "Why can't I see God?" I was referring to the heavenly light that he shielded me from.

"Because no one can see God and live," he answered.

Officer Roy was the first on the scene. "Who do we have here, boys?" A young female, no identification was their answer. Officer Roy bent over the gurney and pulled the sheet away from my face. He cried out, "Oh, God, no! Please, God, not her." He knew some of my story, and he was not about to let me die. He began to administer CPR, and much to the surprise of those standing around, I came back.

I was a miracle! I survived the overdose and the fall. My back was broken, but there was no paralysis; I would be able to walk, and I was alive! The hospital staff tried in vain to reach my parents, but each time they were greeted by Stepdaddy saying, "We have no daughter by that name," and the phone hanging up. I didn't know how to find Angie and had no one else to call. I overheard the nurses talking about sending me to the women's rehabilitation center for minors — on the street I had been told horror stories about that place. I felt so helpless, frightened. *God, please don't let them take me to that awful place; I'll never get out of there.* I lay alone, praying for good news.

Through the door, a tiny black man entered. Our eyes met, and then he moved toward me. He looked as if he had just come from skid row — disheveled and dirty. *Please don't come any closer.* I held my breath slightly, expecting the closer he came that my senses would be invaded by the stench of vomit and urine. Instead, the little man smelled sweet, like fresh-picked flowers. I looked down into his eyes — they were soft, gentle. He opened his mouth and spoke; his words were like music. He said, "I have a message for you from Jesus. He says, 'I am with you now, but I have to leave. And although I have to leave, I will always be with you. And although I will always be with you, I am coming back for you.'" He bent forward, and I closed my eyes as he kissed my face. It was the sweetest kiss I had ever felt. When I opened my eyes, he was gone. *How could he have disappeared so fast?*

A few hours later, a nurse walked in with my discharge papers and said that someone had come for me. I was surprised and delighted to see a kind couple that I had met on the streets — they ran a methadone clinic. "How did you know I was here?" I asked.

"Your guardian angel told us."

I was not at all surprised at their answer.

అతితితి

The tie between a daughter and her daddy is a strong one. Even kidnapping, molestation and murder cannot change that. When Daddy got out of prison, Angie went to live with him, and I went for a visit. Daddy was overprotective and jealous, but the time we spent together was fun, and he showed his delight at seeing me by buying me a car for my 18th birthday. I thought maybe I had finally come home to stay, until one night Daddy got drunk and angry while I was talking to a boy on the phone. Daddy took the phone and threatened to kill the boy, and in his rage, he threatened to kill Mama. I, too, had a lot of anger built up over the past 11 years. I fought back; Daddy swung at me. I ducked, and his hand hit a stud in the wall, shattering every bone. I ran out of the house, and Angie chased after me. "Please don't leave, Caroline. He's just drunk; he didn't mean it."

I jumped in my car. "He did mean it, Angie. He's a murderer, and you should leave with me."

"Daddy won't hurt me; he needs me. I'll be all right," she assured me. I put the car into gear and spun the tires, leaving behind a cloud of dust.

Mama and Stepdaddy were now divorced. *I have to go*

back to LA; I have to protect Mama from Daddy. Mama was not happy to see me. "Caroline, I don't need you to protect me from your father, and I don't want you coming around here anymore."

"But I love you, Mama."

"Well, I don't love you." Then she revealed her true feelings. "I never wanted you," she told me. "I've always hated you." Her words shattered my heart; it finally made sense to me why Mama was so cold and why she never put a name on my birth certificate.

She never wanted me. I am truly an orphan. I have no place to call home, and no one to love me. I left Mama's and lived in my new car for the next year. I used my fake ID to work in bars as a dancer, and I used the money to feed my need to put as many drugs as I could into my body, forgetting all about Jesus and my encounter with death. But Jesus never forgot about me. One night I was drunk and drove my car into a telephone pole, which landed me in jail and got me sober again.

ॐॐॐ

"Hi! I'm Eric. Where you headed?" asked the driver of the Cadillac.

"To my car," I answered, while climbing into the front seat and sinking wearily into the soft leather.

"Where's your car?"

"I'm not sure; all I have are these papers from jail," and I handed them over.

LOST

Eric picked up his car phone and began to dial. *This is my lucky day.*

After a few minutes of driving, he said, "Well, your car is in impound, and it's going to cost money to get it out. I'm headed for Vegas where I have some business meetings to attend. I need a date. Interested? I'll buy you new clothes, and when we get back, I'll help you with your car."

Free food, new clothes and a trip to Vegas sounds good, but at what price? "I'm sorry, but I'm not interested," I said. "I just got out of jail. I've been clean for a few months, and I'm going straight — no more drugs or sex for money. I'm done with that life."

Eric quickly assured me, "It won't be anything like that! I promise!" So, against my better judgment, I trusted him. And, wonder of wonders, it turned out to be true. I enjoyed all the luxuries of the high life while in Vegas — no strings attached. Eric truly was a compassionate man who loved the Lord and hoped to help me.

Eric took me back to LA and gave me a room in his home. He gave me a job with his construction company and a truck. I was so very grateful for all he was doing for me, but I was lonely. When Eric found out I was dating an addict and suspected I was using again, he was furious. I didn't understand his behavior. *Why does he care so much? What does it matter to him, anyway?* When I couldn't hold any food or water down and missed work, Eric thought I was hung over and left me to fend for myself.

IMPOSSIBLE ODDS – HAPPY ENDINGS

I had to get help, and even though I had not talked to Mama for more than a year, I had no one else to turn to. I called Mama and begged, "I need you! Please come pick me up, and take me to the doctor." Much to my surprise, she came. The diagnosis was hepatitis. Mama was willing to get shots so that she could take me home and care for me. She asked me to forgive her and said that she was sorry for not being a good mother. Eric came to visit me on my sickbed, and there he met and fell in love with Mama. Once Mama was convinced that I had never slept with Eric, they started dating.

❧❧❧

I needed money; I asked Mama for parental permission to work in pornography, half hoping that she would say no. But Mama said, "Sure, if that's what you want." *I don't want to; I need money.*

I hated it, and I hated myself for doing it. I was ashamed, and before I knew it, drugs and alcohol became my only solace. I wanted out, to get away, so I took a job working for the movie studios. Living the life of a roadie was long hours and hard work, mixed with drugs and alcohol. It all came to a screeching halt when I overdosed while working. I was rushed to the hospital in Tennessee and released two weeks later, only to get a pink slip. My supervisors told me, "Go to LA. Complete a 30-day treatment program, and then we'll give you your job back."

LOST

Here I go again, God, living on the edge of life and death! I completed my required 30-day treatment but was afraid that if I went back to work, I would start using again, so when I was offered my old job back, I declined. Instead, I took a job waitressing and got engaged to Marcus. We lived happily sober for two years. Mama and Eric got married, and they loved Marcus and welcomed him as a son-in-law. When he cheated on me, I was heartbroken. I called home to find comfort, but Eric's words of wisdom were, "Every man cheats, just forgive him." But I could not forgive; the engagement was off. *What's the use, God? I stay sober, and I'm a good woman to my man, but look at what happens. Is this what I deserve? To be cheated on, abandoned, rejected? I give up.* And I did; I gave up my two years of sobriety for the comfort of a strange man and a bottle.

そうそうそう

The man I met was Ben. He was a carpenter and taught me all about construction. We spent our money on partying, which led to Ben constantly getting arrested and going to jail. We moved from LA to Vegas to get away from the law and to make a new start. We both started going to church, to NA and AA; we served on the prison ministry team together, and we bought a house. Ben encouraged me to go back to school and get my GED, and I graduated!

Mama and Eric had retired and were now living

abroad. They invited Ben and me to come and help them remodel their house. We had never been out of the United States and jumped at the opportunity for adventure. I got pregnant, and we decided to stay abroad and rented a small apartment. Ben asked me to marry him; I answered with a resounding, "Yes!" *This is what I've been hoping and praying for!*

Living abroad was expensive, and life was desolate without the support of our church and sobriety groups. Five weeks after saying, "I do," Ben got an offer to smuggle drugs for a lot of money. It was a temptation that proved too great for him to resist. I thought he was on a legitimate business trip, so when Ben was arrested for international smuggling and sentenced to seven years in a foreign prison, I was devastated. I had never felt so much betrayal in my life. *I am so in love with him. We are going to have a baby. How could he do this to me? God, I can't believe this is happening to me. Please help Ben get out of prison, Lord. I don't want to be a broken family!*

I moved back to the States, where my son, Michael, was born. There I met a woman at a garage sale who shared her love for God with me. She and I became friends quickly. Our church meetings were in her home, and together we all participated in preparing lessons and teaching the Bible. But in the course of a year our church split up. I was distraught and disillusioned about religion. I was struggling to stay faithful to my husband in prison and to help fight for his release, but I never saw Ben again, and the comfort of a man was never far from my mind.

LOST

❧❧❧

When Michael was 3, I moved to Alaska to be close to my best friend and to set about making a new life for myself, which never included finding a new father for Michael. But when I met Tristan a few weeks after I arrived in Alaska, I thought we were meant to be. We decided to have a marriage ceremony in spite of the fact that I wasn't yet divorced from Ben. Five weeks after the wedding, Tristan left me for another man. I felt the very familiar sadness of rejection, but this time the weight of it was heavier because I was pregnant with Tristan's child. I never considered abortion in my life, but I was so sick and in such physical pain from this pregnancy that I could not even take care of Michael. I had to make a choice between caring for the child I had and caring for the child inside of me. Then something inside of me broke. *I can't take this anymore! I can't even take care of the child I have.* In a daze, I traveled to a nearby clinic to get rid of the thing that was breaking me — I had an abortion. *God, I'm sorry. I wanted a sibling for Michael so badly, Lord. I wanted a husband and to be a family! Not this, God. Please forgive me!*

❧❧❧

We found another home fellowship to attend, but soon they began to order people to conform to their rules or else! They kicked out my best friend and her family, and it drove us apart. Then they disclosed how they felt about me and my boyfriend, Bob. "Caroline, if you stay with this man out of wedlock, you are a whore!" *Is that what Jesus thought of me, too?* Their accusing words were sharp and brought back wounds from my teenage days on the streets. I, too, was expelled. I tried to mend my relationship with my best friend, but it would be five long years before we made amends and became best friends again.

When Bob and I did marry, it turned disastrous, too. One night in a drunken rage, Bob beat me up — he busted my ribs and dislocated my shoulder. *I have to save Michael and me.* "Come here, baby," I called to Michael. He bravely moved close enough, and I scooped him up into my arms. I prayed out loud, "In the name of Jesus, back away from me." As I walked closer to the door, I just repeated those words. Every step I took forward, Bob took a step backward, and once I hit the door, I fled for safety to a women's shelter. The police were called, and Bob was arrested for domestic violence. Bob filed for divorce, and I did not contest it. I lost my house and left everything I owned.

ॐॐॐ

With the weight of the world on my shoulders, I sought help in counseling. I was still experiencing the psychosis that started when I was kidnapped, and many other health problems began to rob me of my vitality. The counselors sent me to doctors who gave me drugs. Narcotics for pain, marijuana and muscle relaxers for

LOST

fibromyalgia, bipolar meds for depression, psychotropic drugs for the voices in my head and methamphetamines for narcolepsy; pills to wake up, pills to sleep, pills for diabetes, high blood pressure, chronic bronchitis, asthma and the list went on.

かかか

I could barely work the small construction jobs I was getting because of my injuries. I was physically and emotionally exhausted, with no money and winter quickly approaching. I swallowed my pride and applied for welfare, disability and vocational rehabilitation. I went back to college and at last earned an Associate's Degree.

"Caroline, please come and play drums for us; we need a drummer."

My answer was always the same. "No, and you might as well quit asking me, because I am never going to do it." Sandy would not take no for an answer. So finally I said, "If I come to one rehearsal, will you promise to never ask me again?"

"Yes, I promise," Sandy assured me.

So I went, and when the night was over, the worship leader asked me if I could come back on Sunday to fill in. Before I knew it, I said, "Yeah, sure, if you need me." A little spark inside me ignited; I was excited to play music for the Lord. And so I kept coming back, every week, sometimes high, sometimes sober, to be a part of something that would forever change my life.

IMPOSSIBLE ODDS – HAPPY ENDINGS

৯৯৯

I never missed a Sunday; I loved playing the drums. My heart and mind were changing through the words in the music and from the pulpit. While I was learning to worship Jesus, he was quieting my mind. One morning I woke up, and the psychosis was gone, never to return. After living 30 years in a prison in my mind, I finally had peace. When I praised the Lord, my joy returned to me, and worship took on a whole new meaning.

I could not stay awake on the long commutes to work or at my desk all day. Then the unthinkable happened. I started to buy crystal meth and began snorting it. I was living a double life again, keeping my drug habit hidden from everyone at church, my family and friends. *My existence is a lie. I hate myself!* Before the year was over, I lost my job, my house to foreclosure and my boyfriend left me. *All this loss — I am reaping the wages of my sins!*

"Please, Lord, help me. I want to love you and live my life for you and show people that you are real." It was instant déjà vu; my mind flashed back to a teenage girl standing before Jesus and heaven, asking for her life back. Sorrow flooded my entire being! I flushed all my meth and prescriptions down the toilet, fell to my knees and cried hard. *Jesus, I've tried everything except surrendering to you!*

I SURRENDER!

"Wake up," the preacher's voice rang in my ears, "and fight! I challenge you to fight for your life."

LOST

Oh, Lord, you are talking to me.

I had come so far, but marijuana still had a hold on me and gave me confidence to play drums. I had tried playing sober for months, but every sober practice turned into a train wreck, with the worship leader telling me, "Caroline, play it like you did last week."

Last week I was stoned! Lord, I love playing music, but I want to play sober. I can't seem to do that right now, so today I am laying my drumsticks down at your feet; I present my body to you as a living sacrifice. At the end of the service, I put my sticks down and said, "I quit."

Please, Lord, I need a church where I can be honest and find strength and support. God brought to my mind the Church on the Rock in Palmer. There I found loving people who accepted me as I am and gave me a safe place to be honest. I learned to forgive myself and others and to see myself as Jesus sees me — beautiful! *No more double life, lies or secrets.*

People began to see the change God was creating in me, and one by one it brought them to the Lord; first, my best friend, and soon, Michael and his best friend, then others. My relationship with Angie and Mama and Eric took on new life, as I went through a process of forgiveness with each one of them. God healed our hearts as I was falling in love with Jesus!

Looking back, I can recognize the handprints and footprints of Jesus everywhere throughout my life: the FBI men, Officer Roy, doctors, nurses, a kind man offering a ride with "no strings attached," a stranger at a garage sale,

IMPOSSIBLE ODDS – HAPPY ENDINGS

a friend who invited me to play in a church band and the list goes on. I'm grateful for these good people who showed up to offer me bits and pieces of God's love and who prayed for me. Nothing in God's kingdom ever comes back void, and although it may take some of us longer than others to find our way home, one thing is for certain: It's never too late for a Fresh Start, not for me and not for you.

കൈകൈകൈ

I used to believe the lies I was told. When I looked in the mirror, I would think, *I am so ugly! I am so stupid! I hate my life!* Now I look at myself and see beauty in an intelligent, capable and strong woman of God! My life has purpose — I can be the hands and feet of Jesus. I hid from my past and lived in secrecy, afraid of rejection and criticisms, never realizing that God had a purpose for my journey all along. My story is no longer hopeless. Instead, it has the makings of a really good book, filled with suspense and impossible odds — and a happy ending!

PUSHED

THE STORY OF TRACY
WRITTEN BY ANNE C. JOHNSON

"No," I hollered up to my apprentice, Mike, "you need to push the wire through the conduit first."

Mike was struggling 90 feet above the cold gray pavement of the warehouse trying to pass electrical wire exactly as I wanted it.

"Just wait, I'll be right there."

I climbed the scaffolding we were using to get onto the I-beams that ran the length of the warehouse ceiling. I cautiously stepped onto the sturdy beam. The enormous ceiling crane was clear across the warehouse, so I stepped several feet closer to Mike.

Pulling his harness away from his view, he glanced down at me. His shoulders slumped forward as if this job had defeated him. I wanted to restore his confidence, so I explained more patiently what he needed to do.

I hadn't taken the necessary precautions of strapping a safety harness around me. With the 125-ton ceiling crane more than 100 yards away, I felt confident I would be able to instruct Mike and then descend to the safety of the floor before the monster crane budged from its position.

In midsentence, I felt a strong physical force propel me forward. In my youth, I had lettered in both varsity wrestling and football twice. I knew a shove when I felt

LOST

one. I heard Mike's screams as I lurched forward.

Something odd happens in the split seconds before you meet your demise. My life, like a movie, reeled through my mind.

෴

I was 6 years old when my dad was home from leave for two weeks from the Navy. My sisters and I were sitting on the sofa in the living room watching television.

"Tracy," Dad called, "come here."

My dad demanded attention the moment he spoke because of his military training. Not to mention the man was 6 feet, 3 inches tall and weighed more than 270 pounds. Not the kind of man you want to make mad at you.

I sprung from the couch and hurried to him. He led me outside to the back porch. The sun had begun its slow journey toward the horizon, but in Pleasant Grove, Utah, during the summer, the temperature was still well above 100 degrees.

Dad sat on a lawn chair and placed his enormous hands on my shoulders. As I faced him, my heart skipped a beat. Thoughts swarmed like bees at a hive around my head. I wondered what I had done wrong.

As we were eye to eye, Dad said, "Tracy, I am gone a lot, and when I get out of the Navy next month, I am going to work for your uncle. Do you know what that means?"

PUSHED

I shook my head from side to side, afraid to speak for fear I might say something wrong.

"I'll be driving a semi-truck and won't be around a lot."

"Okay," I muttered. I was used to Dad being gone.

"Now," Dad's hands squeezed my shoulders tighter, "you'll need to be 'the man of the house' for me."

Though Dad wasn't around much, I knew not to ask him questions, so I nodded my head.

"Good," he said and sent me back into the house.

My family roots stemmed back to the early Mormon pioneers who sought religious asylum in Utah. Ninety-five percent of people living in Utah practiced the Mormon faith. The rest were outcasts, shunned for their lack of belief.

My mom, Betty, taught me and my sisters how to embrace our religious convictions. Together, we attended weekly services. As a child, I pressed myself to become the best Mormon I could be, excelling to the highest possible status. After all, I was the man of the house and would need to be an example for my mom and sisters.

"Man of the house." Those words rang in my ears daily. I had no idea how to perform those duties since I didn't have an example to follow. Internally, I decided to be hard, never giving in to tears when I was hurt but rather being stoic and tough, just like Dad.

When I turned 9 years old, my dad found a job that allowed him to be home each night.

My admiration of my dad did a 180-degree turn when

he demanded his role of "man of the house" back.

When Dad settled down into the family routine, he decided we would go to the Temple in Salt Lake City and have our family sealed for eternity. This was a prestigious Mormon ceremony in which dedicated Mormon families participated.

Dressed in my Sunday best, I stood in front of Dad facing the Bishop. The bright white walls around the room seemed to glow with a heavenly presence. The room was silent, anticipating the great event. In awe, I listened to the special prayer said during this ritual that would bind my family together for eternity.

Not long after my dad returned home permanently, he competed against me for everything — Mom's attention, brave deeds done, knowledge about our faith, but most of all for physical activities. Dad proved over and over how he was superior to me, by out-throwing a football, out-hitting a racquetball, pinning me to the ground in less than 30 seconds with simple wrestling moves. The desire to someday beat him at anything pushed me to practice harder.

One Saturday afternoon, I was lying on the couch reading a magazine. My dad came in wearing his gym clothes. I prayed he would keep walking and leave me alone.

"Hey, Tracy, let's go play racquetball," he said.

"Nah."

"Come on, Tracy," Dad coaxed, "I'll take it easy on you."

PUSHED

Sighing, I could feel the grueling task before me. I laid the magazine down and gathered my equipment. We drove to the gym in silence.

Outside the court, I put my safety goggles on, slipped my right hand into the glove, picked up my racquet and headed into the enclosed court. Dad's whoops and hollers echoed off the four walls.

"You got to at least try," he gloated.

I lost the first game 21 to 2. Dad rejoiced in his victory, dancing like a football player who just scored a touchdown. I turned to leave when the words he spoke slammed against me like a ball on the wall. "Giving up," he chuckled. "Guess you're not the man you pretend to be."

Spinning around, I faced him. Heat flooded my face, and resentment filled my heart.

Without a word, the game was on. Sweat poured down my face. I dove for every ball and felt like I tore every muscle in my body in hopes of wiping the smug look off my dad's face. In the end, I lost 21 to 3.

I didn't just lose the game that day; I vowed to never again enter the racquetball court with my dad, Tom. A fire of bitterness and discontent blazed within me toward him. I never verbally called him Tom. I would never dare to show this level of disrespect to him, but by his actions, he had forfeited the title of Dad in my mind.

In junior high, I strove to be the best at everything, pushed by the fervor to prove to Tom I was a better man than he. I swore to myself I would never be like him. I loathed the thought that our family was sealed by the church to spend eternity in heaven.

My internal clock rang as I was riding my bike on the street in front of my house. I peddled furiously into the garage, hung my bike on the proper hook and darted around the house. A moment later, I heard the roar of our family's car pulling into the driveway. From my vantage point at the side of the house, I began my daily ritual of staying outside and listening for Tom's voice. Within 15 minutes or so, if his voice was calm, I would venture into the house. However, if he screamed and yelled at my mom and sisters, I kept my distance until I was called in for dinner. Tom's anger often flared toward us all, but being his only son, I was the only one who received his anger physically.

One summer morning, my mom came into my room. "Hey, sweetie, want to go camping?"

"Is Dad going?" I answered in my customary way.

"Yes," Mom replied.

"Then, no, I'd rather not."

It became Mom's habit to pay me money or buy me something extra to ensure I would go along on outings with the family. My sisters never had the same issue with Tom, and that plagued me.

I pushed myself to excel. I lettered two years in a row, both in varsity wrestling and in varsity football. As a Mormon boy, I reached the designation of priest when I turned 16 years old. I was given the honorable job of breaking and blessing the sacrament bread during every service.

PUSHED

One lazy afternoon, I was lying on the green shag rug watching the *Wide World of Sports* on the television. Tom sat in the La-Z-Boy recliner behind me. Suddenly I felt the force of his 270-pound body slam down on top of me. Though I was startled, my years of wrestling practice paid off. Within 30 seconds, I had flipped Tom and pinned him.

"Betty," Tom screamed, "make the boy get off me!"

My mom poked her head around the corner of the kitchen. "Are you kidding? Tracy's been training for 17 years to do that. Do you think I'm going to stop him now?"

Finally, it was my turn to gloat. Tom moaned. I released him and sat back smiling. Without warning, he jumped on me again. In less time than before, Tom was trapped and begging for help. My hours of practice had gone unnoticed by him, and though I was shorter and weighed less, I was stronger. Discouraged by my two victories and wanting to regain his dominance, he challenged me to an arm wrestling contest. What he didn't know was that I had been challenging a friend of mine to be the first one to curl 200 pounds.

Sitting at the dining room table, Tom faced me. His chin tipped up, and his eyes narrowed. "One, two, three," he counted.

In two seconds, Tom's arm was pinned on the table. After I defeated him two more times, he shoved back his chair, stood and marched out the door. Never again would we compete physically; instead, Tom tried to prove he was still my superior by having the best job, more money and bigger home.

The hatred I had toward him did not compare to the self-loathing I had because of an addiction consuming me since I was 9 — pornography. Not only was this a sin in the Mormon church, but I also despised being controlled by this addiction. And I knew my sin would be discovered someday.

One morning while giving the blessed prayer over the sacred bread at church, I messed up in front of the entire church. I had said this prayer week after week for more than a year. I could say it in my sleep. However, after 13 attempts, my frustration burst forth like a monster from the closet, and I cursed into the microphone. A gasp from my mother was the only sound heard in the stark white church.

A fellow priest jumped up from his wooden pew and came to my rescue. God had finally punished me for my hidden sin. After such a harsh, embarrassing punishment, I vowed never to perform that ceremony again. The childhood picture in my heart about a loving God disappeared that day. Instead, I saw God as an abrasive judge ready to slam down his gavel at my slightest infraction of his unobtainable perfection.

One evening, my mom, sisters and I sat around the dining room table talking. The phone rang. Mom jumped up to answer it. "Oh, Tom, how…" I watched all the color in her face drain. Her body swayed. I rushed to her and stopped her from falling to the floor.

PUSHED

"I can't help," Mom uttered. "No, I won't help!"

Mom stood to her feet. She slammed down the receiver and started down the hall.

"What's the matter?" my sisters chimed in unison.

"Nothing."

Mom's bedroom door slammed before any of us spoke. "So, what do you think Dad did this time?" my oldest sister asked.

"Who cares?" I huffed. "Mom finally stuck up for herself, and that's all that matters."

Mom didn't come out of her room to say goodnight to us. In the morning, the dark circles under her eyes told of her sleepless night. Mom confided in my older sister that Dad had been having an affair with a woman from out of town. He had told Mom that he was going on a business trip, when instead he was going to the graduation of the woman's daughter. He called because he ran out of money to buy bus fare home and wanted Mom to wire him some.

When Tom came home, it wasn't for long. He had ruined the sacredness of marriage and spoiled our eternal family unit. Like gasoline added to fire, flames of hatred seared my heart. I needed comfort and entered into a sinful relationship with my girlfriend, Tammy.

The next bomb dropped into my life when Tammy came over one afternoon with red swollen eyes. My arms weren't enough to comfort her. We sat on the floor in the same spot Tom attempted to wrestle with me one year earlier. The house was empty and still.

I listened to her sobs and held her shaking body.

LOST

"Tammy, please tell me what's wrong."

She pushed me away. Turning her tear-streaked face toward me, she whimpered, "I'm … pregnant."

Worse than being slammed to the floor by a wrestling opponent, I felt the heavy weight of this situation fall upon me. Our parents, friends, priests and elders chastised us. I argued vigorously to keep my child. But our parents forced us to give our baby up for adoption.

The day my son, Josh, was born, I crept into the hospital to peer through the glass window at him in the nursery. Josh was a beautiful boy. Tears formed in my eyes when my son began to cry, and I wasn't able to hold or comfort him.

A dark shadow engulfed my heart. I had failed. This failure added to my public embarrassment at church, and the internal shame of my pornography addiction fertilized the root of depression in my heart.

I finished my robotics degree in one and a half years as the top student in my class. I paid for my tuition by serving in the National Guard. Though I had accomplished these things before my 21st birthday, I still failed to receive Tom's approval. So I pushed myself even harder.

After securing a job as an apprentice at a large construction firm in Utah, I felt honor bound to marry Tammy. Though she had been baptized at age 8 in the Mormon church, she and her family weren't practicing any form of religion. In fact, Tammy was against organized religion due to being shunned by the whole

PUSHED

Mormon community where we grew up. In Utah, if you weren't Mormon, you were a nobody.

Tammy's dad suffered from pornography addiction, also, so when my new wife found out my secret, she allowed me to practice it openly. For Christmas one year, she bought me a couple of subscriptions.

I wished our marriage was one of peace as an eternal family should be, but there was great tension and turmoil between Tammy and me. We had three wonderful children, and as with everything, I desired to be the best dad possible. However, thanks to my poor role model, I felt like a failure as a parent.

One night after a severe quarrel with Tammy, I stormed out of the house. I drove around trying to decide what my next move would be. I hated my life. And at that moment, I hated Tammy. I spotted a friend's car at an all-night restaurant and figured at least I'd have company. There was a woman among us who I found easy to talk to, and in the morning, I found myself wrapped in her arms.

The sun's rays colored the sky an amazing pink, a color not found in any box of crayons. On a typical day, I may have offered a prayer of thanks for such a sight. However, the darkness that filled my heart for years now consumed me. I had failed as a husband. As I parked my car in front of my house, I looked at my reflection. I strived to be better than Tom my entire life. But step by step, I mimicked the man I loathed, going to the same college, getting the same degree, cheating on my wife, destroying my family's eternal status and being a second-rate dad.

LOST

What excuse was I going to give Tammy? Walking toward the house, I tried to think back to a time when I was happy and not engulfed by a cloud of despair. I stepped inside, saw the kids on the floor and instantly remembered church. Tammy came around the corner, her hands resting on her hips.

"Well," she demanded.

"I've been thinking, I think we need to start going to church."

"You go," Tammy said through clenched teeth, "but I'll have no part of it."

She stayed true to her word. For weeks, I dragged the kids to church with me, trying desperately to rekindle my happiness. Tammy's anger burned hotter toward me, so one night I packed my suitcase and walked out.

ॐॐॐ

These scenes flashed before my eyes as my body lurched forward. Hopelessly I grabbed for the vertical column three feet away. My hands pressed against the metal beam. And by some miracle the heels of my work boots snagged on the I-beam I had been standing on.

The beam vibrated as the enormous ceiling crane brushed the fluff on the back of my jacket. I felt a slight pressure but nothing compared to the impact I would have felt if I hadn't been shoved from behind.

Mike was able to hook a cable to the safety harness I wore and hoist me back up onto the I-beam.

PUSHED

"What kind of stupid stunt was that?" Mike hollered after we were both on solid ground.

"I didn't do it," I stammered. "I was pushed."

"By what? We are 90 feet up in the air."

"I don't know — God?"

"Whatever; I think we best call it a day," Mike sighed.

I drove home shaken, not by the fall, but by the powerful presence I felt shove me out of the way of the crane. At the instant I was pushed a feeling of peace and love swept through me, and just as quick as it was there it was gone again. Had I experienced a physical touch from God? Whatever it was, I wanted more.

After our divorce was final, I plunged into studying to be ordained as an Elder in the Mormon church. I worked full time and went to ministry classes at night. I began taking part in ceremonies at the Temple. One of my official jobs was to prepare young men to go into the field to witness to the non-Mormon — the lost.

During my schooling to become an Elder, I met and married Tonya. She believed faith was the key to a happy life and marriage. We had two sons, Sam and Andrew, were happy attending the Mormon church and were striving to work hard to please God.

While I was in ministry school, I had made a vow to avoid pornography, but like any addiction, without support and accountability the desire to have a fix was overwhelming.

Not only had I succumbed to my fleshly desires, a wedge formed between my faith and my selfish nature. I also noticed Tonya pulling away from the church. She began to schedule her shifts for every Sunday.

"Why aren't you going to church, Mommy?" my littlest boy asked one time.

"I can't be good enough, so why try?"

"What?" I stammered. My sons and I watched her grab her purse and stomp out the front door.

I continued my pursuit for happiness by deepening my involvement in the church. One class I taught was to novice missionaries on how to deal with problematic interviewees. We role-played different situations where the students learned to interview a hostile non-Mormon. For weeks the kids came to class faced with difficult questions I had formulated to stump them as they practiced witnessing to me. However, I, too, became confused by conflicts I found between the words in the Bible and Joseph Smith's teachings.

The biggest question I struggled with centered around one of the core beliefs in Mormonism, the eternal family. I was taught that Joseph Smith, the founder of the Mormon church, received a revelation from God concerning the ceremonial sealing of a married couple and family for eternity. However, one day I read in Mark 12:25 where some religious teachers questioned Jesus about seven brothers who died and had been married to the same woman and none of them had kids. The teachers asked Jesus whose wife she would be in heaven. Jesus replied, "When the dead rise, they will neither marry nor be given in marriage; they will be like the angels in heaven." So in

PUSHED

my mind either the Bible lied or Joseph Smith lied about marriages in heaven.

When I sought the counsel of my bishop, I was told I wasn't a devoted Mormon nor educated well enough on the doctrine of my faith.

Angered by his response and confused by such questions as the eternal family, I turned away from religion once again. I had given five years of my life in service to the church, only to be let down again. Like a tornado in my mind, thoughts of failure, worthlessness and inadequacies swirled.

I needed to get away from my mom, the Mormon church, everything. Tonya had been raised in Alaska and had always wanted to return, and so we did.

One night when I walked into the house, I found Tonya face down on the couch bawling. Spread out on the floor laid my dirty magazines. My legs trembled as I stepped toward the couch.

"I —"

"Shut up!" she hollered. "I hate you. How could you do this to me?"

"I'm sorry."

I was sorry, but the damage was done. The pain I caused her went to the core of who she was. Never again would I have her trust.

Though we tried counseling, it did not help. We fought terribly; at times I was consumed with anger. I decided to stay in a motel for a month to give us space to think. I discovered through our oldest son that Tonya had invited her boyfriend over to spend the night the day after I moved into the motel.

Divorce number two. Finally, I had beaten Tom at something. Sitting in my small one-room apartment, I reached for my pistol. I stared at the dark round chamber. "Why not?" I asked, my voice echoing in my sparsely decorated room. There were no thoughts, no feelings, no questions, just blackness. As I raised the gun to my head, the phone rang.

For some odd reason, I answered. "Yeah."

"Hey, Dad, it's Sam."

It was Sam, my son. I lowered the pistol onto my lap.

"Dad?"

"Yeah, I'm here."

"Hey, just wanted to wish you a happy birthday."

Wow, he had remembered. I hadn't even remembered. I quickly did the math and realized it was my 37th birthday.

"So, what's up?" Sam asked.

We had a great talk, and by the end of the night there seemed to be a pinpoint of light in the blackness that earlier seemed to have swallowed me whole.

The light didn't last long. The next week at work my boss called me into his office. I had made a drastic mistake in the electric plans I had drawn up, and if he hadn't discovered the error, it could have been catastrophic.

It was not the first time my work had been scrutinized, but my boss was gracious and asked if there was anything he could do to help.

PUSHED

Since I had moved to Alaska, I had taken up the sport of competitive shooting. I had several guns, and living alone, there wasn't any reason not to keep the magazine clips to the guns around.

After work that night, I scoured my apartment for my bullets. I tore the place apart but could not find them. I sat down and cried. For the first time since I walked away from my firstborn son, I sobbed. *What have I done with my life? Who am I?* These questions resounded in my mind. Never in my life had I felt so lost, so alone.

I hated being alone, so I tried Internet dating — how else do you find girls when you're almost 40 years old? One time while on the computer, I received a message on my profile. The woman's name was Amy. My heart raced when I discovered such a lovely lady lived in the same town.

For our first meeting, I suggested a cute diner/café where we could eat breakfast. I met Amy at her car and opened the door for her. Walking into the brightly lit diner, we were greeted by the smell of frying bacon, eggs and strongly brewed coffee. The waitress bustled by us, arms laden with plates. She returned moments later and led us to a booth at the back of the diner. I sat across from Amy and noticed how blue her eyes were. They reminded me of a blue cat's eye marble I had as a boy. It was easy to find things to talk about, like the regular morning crowd, the clanging sounds of a busy kitchen, the amusing waitress and the hope of spring budding on the Alaska landscape.

LOST

For our second date, Amy invited me to a meeting hosted by her church. I wanted to spend time getting to know her and was drawn to the joy I saw in her eyes and heard in her voice. But as I rode to this meeting she called "Fresh Start," an internal battle raged within me. *How could I, a Mormon, attend a Christian function?*

The meeting was held at Amy's church. There were a lot of people there, and they greeted me and seemed to be genuinely happy that I was there; I felt a sense of warmth I had never experienced. Not physical warmth, but a deep inner peaceful sensation.

The leader prayed, then announced the speakers for the night. A couple sitting across the room from Amy and I began to share their story about infidelity in their marriage, their debt and many other issues they had faced.

As I listened, I thought how messed up these people were. Yet, really, who was I to talk?

Wrapping up their testimony, they declared if it had not been for their faith in God and the support of the congregation from Church on the Rock, they would have divorced years ago.

"Wow," I said to Amy as we walked out the front door.

"Did you like it?"

"Well, I don't know what to think, really."

Amy asked, "Want to go to church with me Sunday?"

No! My mind screamed in a voice that sounded like my mom's. I was glad for the darkness that softly blanketed us, because I was sure Amy would laugh at my dreadful expression. My heart raced, my stomach clenched and I fought to breathe normally. *I must say no. I couldn't betray my family, my faith and my…* I glanced at Amy's face while holding the car door open for her. "Yes, I'd like to go to church with you."

I enjoyed listening to Amy's stories on the drive to her home. Even the tragic story of her husband, who died of cancer two years earlier and left her to raise four children alone, was told with a sense of hope and peace.

Once back in the security of my apartment, I wrestled with the thoughts of betraying my Mormon upbringing. But in the end I realized Amy and the couple who shared their testimony that night possessed what I wanted, what I had searched for my entire life — true happiness.

Amy picked me up on Sunday morning with her van full of giggling children. I had met the kids before and liked their silly antics. Walking across the parking lot toward the church, it seemed the entire universe stopped. The birds were silent; even Amy's kids were quiet. "No," a small voice whimpered in my mind.

I reached out and grabbed Amy's hand. Together we entered the lobby of the church. It was filled with people. This gray-haired man, with a big smile on his face, grabbed my hand, shook it and gave me a hug. After he released his embrace, he exclaimed, "Hi! I'm Pastor Gary, and I'm glad to see you could join us here at Church on the Rock." Gary hugged all the kids, then the kids immediately ran off to see their friends. My mind was still trying to figure out why this old man had given me such an earnest embrace, when Amy led me to the sanctuary. As I walked through the open set of double doors, what seemed like a familiar presence rushed toward me.

Had I not been holding onto Amy's hand, I might have fallen over backward. Sitting in the burgundy seats, staring at the dim stage lights, I marveled at the presence of peace warming the room. There was something about this feeling that was filling my soul. I knew this feeling, but what was it?

As the worship team began to sing praises to God, I felt the connection deep inside. My memory brought me back to that instant when I was pushed out of the way from the bridge crane that nearly took my life 11 years earlier. The feeling of the presence of God once again filled my soul. I knew I was now home, and I would never leave his presence again.

Pastor David Pepper spoke the word of God with authority and passion. Amens echoed around the room. I hated leaving that charged yet serene place. Amy introduced me to some of her friends, and when they asked if I enjoyed the service, I fought to control my excitement.

The next week dragged as I longed to return to the warm presence I had felt at Church on the Rock. The worship music was contemporary, and I found it easy to follow along. The words the pastor spoke were both healing and convicting. At the end of the service, Pastor David asked us all to stand, close our eyes and bow our heads. With my eyes closed, I could hear the pastor speak, my heart was beating strong and I felt alive, something I had not felt for all my adult life. I can still hear his words now.

"I feel there is someone here who has been struggling to find truth, searching to find what was lost. If that is you, please raise your hand."

There was a whisper in my ear from an unknown voice. "That was you; raise your hand." Slowly I raised my hand.

"Is there someone here who wishes to dedicate his or her life to our Lord Jesus Christ today? Please raise your hand." That day, Pastor David invited us to pray and ask Jesus Christ into our lives. I responded by raising my hand and praying with him.

Immediately lights burst through the blackness twisted around my heart. From then on I would have God's presence with me. I was freed from a 21-year history of clinical depression and antidepressant use, and my addiction to pornography vanished.

For months, Amy helped me understand the conflicts I had with scripture and the teaching of Joseph Smith. By sharing with me all the notes she had taken on Pastor Pepper's sermons and reading the Bible together, I began to see faith is not just believing in God but also daily choosing to serve him.

Two months after I began my new relationship with Jesus Christ, David called me from Utah inviting me to his graduation from high school. I learned in the Fresh Start class I was attending with Amy that to really feel free from past bondages, I had to trace the source of my sin back to the past. Through prayer, I determined I had to get rid of the animosity toward Tom.

On the flight to Utah, I rehearsed the words I would say to Tom. I knew I had to confront him. Driving to my older sister's house was tedious, not because of traffic or the flashback of memories that assailed me, but because my heart felt squeezed. A feeling like I was about to do something terrible pursued me. I started to pray as I pulled into the driveway.

The graduation was wonderful, and though I tried endless times to snag a few minutes alone with Tom, it never materialized. Heading to the airport, my old friend, failure, tried to hook its claws into me once again.

My cell phone rang as I zoomed down the freeway. I answered without looking at the caller ID.

"Tracy, it's your dad," the caller said.

"Hey."

Since I had moved out of the house 20 years before, I only called Tom when a new grandchild was born. We never talked, because I had nothing to say to him.

"I ... I," his voice cracked.

"You all right?"

"I'm proud of you," Tom blurted out. "I love you, son. I don't think you know how much I love you."

The road blurred through the deluge of my tears. I steered my rental car off to the side of the road. I listened as Tom inundated me with compliments and tender thoughts.

"I love you, too, Dad," I said before hanging up.

PUSHED

On the airplane ride back I sat in a window seat. The aircraft climbed out of the clouds, and instantly my face was bathed in light. What an awesome visual to the light that exploded within my heart. I wanted to burst into the aisle of the plane and dance. I was free. Bitterness, failure and anger had fallen off me like skin from a molting snake.

After I returned from my trip, members of my Fresh Start class asked me what had happened. "You're not the same," everyone said. "Your countenance isn't dark anymore."

I celebrated with my church family about the restoration of my relationship with my dad. The first major issue in my life had been processed successfully, thanks to God's gentle leading. During my prayer one night, I felt God's gentle presence fill my apartment. There were other major issues in my life I needed to deal with. My failed marriages and the surrendering of my firstborn son were tremendous sources of pain. I decided to deal with the sins surrounding my failed marriages.

On my 41st birthday, David called.

"Hey, Dad. I just wanted to be the first to say happy birthday."

"Thanks. I appreciate the call. How are things?"

"You sitting down?"

"Uh, no. Do I need to?"

The pause in the conversation was my answer. "Okay, I'm sitting down," I offered.

"Have you heard from Josh yet?"

"Who?"

LOST

"My older brother," David replied.

"You don't have an—" The light bulb in my mind turned on. Questions flooded my mind. *How? When? Where?*

David didn't have many details, just that Tammy had put a notice on an adoption site about the details of Josh's birth, and while searching the Internet, Josh had replied. David offered me Josh's Facebook information before we ended our call.

Stunned, I lay back against the couch and closed my eyes. It was just like God to work on the hardest issues in my life first. And how remarkable that after all these years, Josh reached out to us! In our conversations via the computer, I finally had the answer to the question that has plagued me for years — Josh has had a happy life.

The healing process in my life continues. God has faithfully restored my relationship with my dad and has brought my son back to me. I still am a very driven man, pushing to know and understand all I can about God and growing in my relationship with him. As I lead a Fresh Start class and a marriage support class with my new wife, Amy, I marvel at how God's presence was woven intricately into my life.

In my life I have made some bad choices, but God has been able to utilize my mistakes. I am using my experiences, the good and the bad, to teach others how to deal with the pains and mistakes in life. My testimony is stronger because of the many things God has been able to heal me of and help me through. Hoeing out the roots of

PUSHED

animosity, bitterness and depression would have been impossible apart from my relationship with God. I still have many issues from the past to deal with, but with God's help, I will continue to push forward, rejoicing in the new life I have been given — a Fresh Start.

THE DANCE PARTNER
THE STORY OF TYE ZALESKI
WRITTEN BY CHRISTEE WISE

My son and two daughters, like silent robots, moved around their bedrooms tossing leftover belongings into suitcases and boxes. I passed Alan's door and noticed my college-bound 18 year old sitting on the floor, back to the wall, staring at an open duffel bag. I didn't stop. There was nothing left to say that hadn't already been said.

Yesterday, I hugged him and told him how proud I was of him. "Alan, I'm sorry I won't be there to help you get started at school."

"It's really not a big deal, Mom." He squeezed my shoulders in return. "I'll just be happy to get there and get started. And you have the girls to think of. I just want you to be happy."

When did this man take over my little boy's body?

I just want you to be happy, Mom. His words lifted me and haunted me at the same time. He echoed my thoughts exactly: *I just can't wait to get there and get started.*

After months of turmoil, my husband, Ben, made a final attempt to change my mind. "Tye, I don't want you to go. Are you sure this is what you want?"

For an instant I wanted to stop the movers. I wanted to look at Ben, tell him there was hope and to know in my heart that we could be happily married forever after all.

LOST

I turned from my fantastical thinking and focused my attention on the boxes in our front room. His and Alan's things were marked "Paris, Tennessee." Those with my name, "Jillian" or "Gabrielle" would go to Wilmington, North Carolina. I took a deep breath and tightened my ponytail, dividing it into two handles that I yanked to slide the band back toward my scalp. Then I unconsciously reached down with both hands to pinch the hem of my t-shirt and pull it over the back of the waistband of my pants. Because my clothes fit snugly, the knit fabric of my tops crept up around my ribs, especially when I'd been moving and lifting.

I wish I'd lost some weight for my new job, I thought. The reminder of the start date just a week away suddenly gave me the resolve to keep separating the household goods for the movers. The Lord had clearly provided the job in Wilmington that was above and beyond what I needed to support myself and the girls.

No, the unhappy marriage was over, and it was time to move on. Hopefully, I could go back to the South and start again.

હેલ્લેલ્લેલ્લે

The bathroom door closed more loudly than I usually allowed, with a wham and a click and a slight rattle. I lunged toward the counter, jerking and slamming the drawer and cabinet to gather my toiletries. Had Mother heard the banging, she'd have corrected me sharply. No worry of that. The noise I made helped me drown out the rest and concentrate on my preparation for the all-day dance clinic. The clinic promised to be my escape the rest of the day.

The bathroom isolation chamber raised an inadequate barrier to my parents' incessant arguing. They were going at it in the kitchen, Dad hollering about Mom's nagging or spending or who knew what and Mom shouting a laundry list of his shortcomings.

I tuned out, humming a new country tune I'd heard on the radio and enjoying the pleasant sound and feel of warm water bursting from the showerhead. World War III was still going on when I got out, but I focused all of my attention on drying and fixing my hair. I turned the lavender comb to use the pointy end to make a part in my hair. Carefully taking aim, I practically sliced my head with the tip in attempt of a precisely straight line my mother would inevitably require upon inspection — best to get it right. After only two tries, I triumphed. My breath, which I'd been holding, came out with a sigh.

Nine-year-old Darryll, my brother three years my junior, and I endured a tense breakfast and marched toward our next appointments in compliance with strict but unwritten house rules.

"Thank you," I spoke with appropriate volume and respect when we pulled up to the dance academy.

A deeply disguised sense of relief surfaced in simple joy when I hopped out of the car. Closing the car door behind me and swinging the glass door wide open in front

LOST

of me, I left my cares behind and walked into the dance studio.

I was born to dance. My escape in it was thorough.

Tap, pointe, jazz, ballet, acrobatic. My mother enrolled me in my first class when I was 3. By the time I was 12, I was one of the best in Louisiana. In spite of my tendency toward perfectionism, I somehow abandoned myself in the world of dance. Dance was my savior.

Everything else, the way I dressed, did my hair, the grades I made, friends and activities, were rigorously monitored. Although I tried and tried to meet the standard, with each achievement the bar moved higher, and I fell short. I never knew which area of my life might come under scrutiny next, only that there'd always be something that wasn't quite perfect.

I awoke regularly to my clothes laid out for me. Throwing back the covers, I got up and stripped off my nightgown. Trying to cover myself with my left arm, I reached for my underclothes. Suddenly the door burst open.

I jumped in surprise and gave a little shriek.

"For pity's sake, Tye, it's just me." My mother bustled into the room.

"Sorry," I responded half-heartedly. Mother was already opening the drawers to my dresser. My nerves remained attentive, though I inwardly reassured myself that I had not changed the contents of my dresser drawers since the last confrontation.

"Are your things straight?" she demanded.

I dared not respond. *Of course, they are. You straightened them the day before yesterday.*

She plopped a short stack of meticulously folded dance leotards and t-shirts on top of the chest. "Put these away…" she paused and then added, "correctly. And come down to breakfast."

I stood dumbfounded and half-naked. When I said nothing, she turned to look me up and down from the wide-open doorway. "Your hair looks awful."

My heart sank with discouragement. I hadn't even had a chance to run a brush through the hairdo a night's sleep had managed. But I could never do my hair well enough to please my mother, anyway. At least she hadn't commented on my weight as she often did when she saw me without clothes.

"Too bad you got your features from your father," she clucked about my appearance.

I couldn't see the resemblance. For a while, I simply dismissed the curse on my beauty that she credited to my father's side. I couldn't push the comments away as easily when I entered that terribly awkward pre-teen period. I was not as pretty as my classmates and would never be so.

Nor was I truly capable of properly cleaning my room.

One horrible day, I approached our house on my way home from school and spotted something unusual on our front lawn. From a distance it looked like a mound of linens waiting to be hung on the line, which we didn't have, or to spread out for a picnic, which we never had, either. Then, as I drew closer, to my horror, I recognized

LOST

the items in the mound. My clothing: My shirts, underwear, dance tights, the entire contents of my dresser had been dumped in a pile in the front yard for the whole world to see. I imagined more than heard my classmates' surprised gasps and giggles. My face burned with embarrassment, and I rushed to the house unable to stifle sobs of angry hurt.

Still, I wondered what I'd done wrong. *I put those clothes in the drawers just as she had folded them, exactly as she had them arranged.*

Even after this humiliating incident, I kept trying to please. But stirring beneath the drive to be an excellent student and an elite dancer was an agonizing fear that I'd never measure up. I became so adept at hiding my insecurities that even I failed to recognize my codependence.

My brother and I weren't strong-willed or rebellious. I think after a while we saw our parents' absence as a blessing. We accepted the responsibility of being home alone with appreciation for the peace that came with it. The rest of the time we tried our best to go with the flow. Unfortunately, the flow was often unpredictable.

Mother was working, and Dad hadn't come home. I fixed dinner for the two of us, and we finished our homework. Darryll had gone to bed, and I fell asleep on the couch.

Much later, my father shuffled in and collapsed in his La-Z-Boy. He'd been drinking. His shirt had come untucked, and he'd loosened his belt.

THE DANCE PARTNER

"Sis, go get me some chicken," he slurred the order over his shoulder at me.

I glanced at the clock. It was well after midnight on a weeknight. I wanted to duck out of the room, pretend that I didn't hear him. Nothing was open in our small town, let alone a chicken place.

"Din-cha hear me?" he arched his back and bellowed from his throne. "Go get me some chicken!"

"Dad, it's after midnight." I tried to keep my voice even. The ink was barely dry on my driver's license. I was more terrified of having a wreck, being stranded on the remote country highway or doing something wrong and getting a ticket than I was of making a B in Chemistry.

"So? I want some Church's Fried Chicken," he demanded.

"But, Dad, Church's is in Lake Charles. That's 20 miles, and it's the middle of the night. They probably aren't even open."

My father rocketed out of the chair, nearly falling as he tried violently to kick the footrest back. His face was red with boozing and effort. His eyes bulged. "How dare you give me lip, you little…" His belt swooshed and cracked loudly when he yanked it from the waistband and loops of his pants in one menacing motion. The sound punctuated the ugly name he called me.

I was raised to be respectful, to do as I was told, to let my elders determine what was right and wrong for me. Fighting my father, running, crying for help were never options for me. I stood stock still with indecision.

LOST

When I graduated from high school, dance gave me a way out. I left home immediately to join a prestigious dance group in New York for a season.

Six months later, I returned to Sulphur and landed a job in Lake Charles at a 50s and 60s dance club called Chevy's. Walking into Chevy's was like walking onto the set of *Happy Days*. Someone was always hand-feeding the original jukebox with coins, punching the colored buttons that brought it to life. Then they'd watch it shuffle the big black discs like a mechanical Atlantic City dealer. The music played, and no one could sit still. I taught them the Twist and the Jitterbug and the Mashed Potato.

Chevy's was also a perfect venue for meetings of the Classic Car Club. The club's president, Ben Zaleski, spotted a couple jitterbugging together across the floor.

Shoving his elbow into his vice president's ribs, Ben leaned over and asked him, "You see that girl right there?" motioning with a soft drink toward where we were dancing.

Ben's friend followed his line of sight to me. He jerked his chin in recognition, and Ben said, "I am going to marry that girl."

The friend laughed and pummeled Ben playfully with his fists. "Yeah, man. And we'll have that rusty old 57 Chevy ready for a show first. Dreamin', man; you're dreamin'."

They were both right. Several weeks went by before Ben and I actually met, and my interest was minimal. He was infinitely patient. He simply refused to give up until I agreed to go out with him. We were quite compatible, sharing the same faith, values and interests and even dreams.

"Ya' know what?" I wondered aloud as we passed a travel agency, its front window plastered with posters of exotic destinations.

"What?" Ben played along.

"Someday I'd like to go to Alaska," I finished.

"Really," Ben answered. "Me, too. You think you'd ever want to live there?"

"Why not?" I replied nonchalantly.

After that we talked about Alaska many times, imagining how and why and when we might get there together.

As newlyweds we settled in Lake Charles and after a couple of years began our family. Our firstborn was Alan. When he was 3, his sister, Jillian, was born, and our youngest, Gabrielle, came along a few years later. I continued to dance and to teach dance; I had significant connections in the dance community, as well as working in an office.

We'd been married 16 years when Ben took a new job in Minnesota. We found a house and made new friends quickly. Our children were young enough that they adjusted easily and began to thrive. Alan entered high school; Jillian would soon follow. Gabrielle loved school, too.

Most important to us was to find a church home. Ben and I had both been Christians most of our lives. When I

LOST

was young, a local church brought a bus to our neighborhood to pick up kids who wanted to go to Sunday school. My brother and I were regulars, though our parents rarely showed interest in church. When I was 12, I accepted Jesus as my Savior. Ben had come to believe in the Lord Jesus at an early age, and we agreed to raise our children to know Christ as well. Very soon after arriving in Big Lake, Minnesota, we found ourselves involved in a local fellowship that we enjoyed very much.

Once we moved, the distance stretched between myself and the oppressive criticism of my youth and set our new place apart. The freedom of choice and self-direction was an exhilarating and intoxicating new experience for me.

I paid little attention to my thickening body except to breathe a sigh of relief that Mom wasn't there to tell me I was getting fat. The relentless criticism had continued after Ben and I had gotten married. I didn't decorate my house well enough or keep it clean enough. My parenting wasn't right. And my hair and makeup were always a source of concern.

When I was growing up, we had summers off from dance. I always missed the diversion of dancing, but I relaxed and found other things to enjoy. My body changed, and my weight often fluctuated as much as 25 pounds between winter and summer. When I reached my full height of 5 feet, 4 inches in high school, I trimmed down to a healthy 130 pounds, mostly solid muscle, during the winter and plumped up in the summertime.

Having spent virtually my entire life in the Lake

Charles area in the discipline of dance, I'd built relationships within the dance community that were closer than family. I taught in the same academy at which I trained and coached school dance teams where I had gone to school.

Then we moved to the Midwest. For the first time in many years, I was no longer dancing every day. I was happy to be coaching the high school dance team a couple times a week, and I kept busy with our children's school and church activities. Each time I thought about the weight gain, I looked in the mirror and gave myself a little positive self-talk: "I don't look half-bad for a 30-something mother of three."

Why am I so unhappy? The question kept popping into my mind.

A dark, heavy depression crept in on me like a fog, inch by inch, swirling in my thoughts more and more each day. I couldn't push it away, and it pressed down on me, multiplying my burden like the extra pounds I gained one by one.

My husband never commented on my weight. He rarely complained about anything. We never fought or argued. All five of us were happy participants of a solid Bible-teaching church for most of three years.

Ben's job in Big Lake neared its end. High school graduation approached for Alan. And I grew more and more restless and unhappy. Each day, I got up with less enthusiasm than I had the day before.

"I've found a position in Tennessee," Ben announced.

LOST

"How'd you like to live in Nashville?"

My spirit lifted a little at the thought of moving to the Country Music Capitol. I loved to sing, and the thought of performing sparked some excitement. But soon the spark began to sputter, dampened by heavy discontent.

The alarm went off early in the morning, but I allowed it to buzz for a full 30 seconds before I could heave myself from under the covers. "I just don't care anymore," I groaned aloud. Ben stepped out of my way and stood by, concerned but helpless.

I staggered into the bathroom expecting to hurry through my morning routine and avoid the mirror as I'd been doing for weeks. But something caused me to pause, and I gasped at my reflection. My hands flew to my mouth as I stared at the fat woman in the mirror. "Oh, my Lord," I breathed.

In a single instant, two revelations swept into my conscience with dizzying impact. My marriage was a wreck, and I was huge. I couldn't go on like this. But what was I to do?

Earnestly, I prayed that God would show me the way out.

My friend Teresa was bursting with news.

"I got a job in North Carolina. I'm moving back down near my family," she blurted over the phone.

I felt myself sway a little as I let her news sink in. We were moving to Tennessee very soon, but her announcement struck a chord.

As she spilled the details, I began to turn an idea over

in my mind. *If Teresa can make a choice to do something like this and just start over, why can't I? In fact, I could just go with her, and I'd know at least one person.*

The more I thought about it the more I thought this had to be the answer. I prayed, "Lord, please show me what you want. Please stop me from making a mistake."

Later in the week, my phone rang with a call that confirmed to me God's clear direction.

The woman identified herself as the Human Resources Director with whom I'd spoken a few days earlier. I'd called to inquire about jobs in the North Carolina branch of a company I'd worked for in Louisiana.

"It so happens," she continued in a professional tone, "that we do have an opening for which we think you are very well suited. We'd like to offer you an associate position in our branch here in Wilmington."

"Really?" My face grew warm as I realized how impressed and interested I sounded.

"Yes. I am going to send you the offer letter, but I think you will be pleased to know that we're offering significantly more, around 5 percent more, than you indicated you would need."

"Really?" Now I was stunned. *This must be a sign,* I thought.

"Ms. Zaleski?"

My imagination led me on a field trip into my future.

"Ms. Zaleski? Are you interested?"

"Oh, yes. Yes, I'm interested." My mind scrambled back to the present. "Yes," I repeated, stalling to arrange my thoughts, "but I'm going to need a few days to uh … to … think it over and put things in order."

Ben was stunned. "What are you doing?"

"I've got a job in North Carolina," I stated simply. "I'm going to move back there."

His face was filled with confusion and pain. "But why? We can work this out. Just tell me what's wrong, and we'll figure it out."

"Our marriage…" I started to explain and stopped to find words. "I'm just unhappy in the marriage."

Still in shock, he repeated the question, "But why? I love you with all my heart, Tye. What do you need?"

"Nothing. It's just that the marriage isn't working." I left it at that for lack of a concrete explanation for my unhappiness.

The decision came as a complete shock to all of our friends and family. For the first time in my life, I had made a decision not to just go with the flow, but to take control of my life. How could I explain that I wanted to take this leap of faith because I sensed the Lord's blessing? Things fell into place at every turn right up to moving day.

There were many tears from the girls as we headed down the highway. They, too, had assured me of their desire for me to be happy, but I knew that moving away from their dad was hard for them. It wasn't until we arrived, began to make friends and to settle into the new job, home and school that I could embrace a new sense of freedom. It was like leaving my parents' house and stepping into the dance world. For several weeks, I enjoyed the same abandonment I felt when I gave myself over to music and movement.

"I'm in control," I said aloud to myself, pausing in front of the mirror as I prepared for my new job. The trim and happy dancing bride was gone, replaced by a nearly 300-pound single woman. With sickening honesty, I had to admit, "No, Tye, you are completely *out* of control."

I found a qualified nutritionist almost immediately and began to retrain myself. Knowing the support of Christian fellowship was crucial, we located a church right away. Soon I found a support group for studying the Bible and making specific application to struggles and hurts in life. I found myself growing in my Christian faith as never before. I discovered new freedom in surrendering to Christ and relinquishing control of areas of my life to him.

On almost every plane, my life began to improve. The weight was coming off spiritually, as well as physically. Between the work I did with the nutritionist and the support of the church group, God revealed that I had a wrong idea of my identity. *I am not defined by my weight or by my appearance or by what I do or don't do well. God loves me unconditionally.*

My heart absorbed the new messages with gratitude. I gained momentum to tackle the bitterness and unforgiveness I harbored in my heart toward my parents. The relationship with my parents improved, yet another confirmation that I was on the right track with the Lord in separating. Confident in this new direction, I began to research and move forward with the divorce proceedings.

LOST

"Is this really what you want?" Ben asked.

"Yes," I replied, hoping my voice sounded neither too firm nor too soft. "I think we need to just make a clean break … get a fresh start."

Ben was quiet for a moment. "How are the girls?"

"They are okay. They miss their friends, but they are doing pretty well. I think they like the church." I tried to be positive and confident. Wanting to comfort him, I added, "They miss you."

"I miss them, too," he mused. "And I miss you."

Finally he concluded, "I don't want a divorce. But if that is what you want, I am not going to fight it. I just want you to be happy. Whatever you want, it's yours."

My pride assailed me. I was much like the bride who has misgivings but goes through with the wedding because the invitations have been sent and the guests are arriving. In my case, though, I was dissolving the union. Nevertheless, I was compelled to complete what I had set in motion. All of the hurt and pain I'd caused the family already, all of the unhappiness I left behind, all of the confirmation I'd had in leaving the marriage and now the improvements I felt — I couldn't simply undo this thing. I must finish it.

With no contest from Ben, the paperwork for the divorce sailed through the system not quite one year after we'd left Minneapolis.

Jillian and Gabrielle were terribly unhappy in North Carolina. I soon decided it was best to take them back to Minnesota where we could renew friendships. I continued my discipline to get fit and also to grow in my faith by studying the Bible with other Christians. I clearly needed to learn how to hear God's direction in my life. My quest to know God in a personal way was satisfied with outpourings of love and forgiveness that I felt in my times of prayer. The unconditional love and forgiveness the Lord poured out to me prompted me to extend it to the ones who had caused me to feel unlovable. I flew to Louisiana one week to spend time with my parents. I carefully explained the transformation in my life and told them I would not carry bitterness toward them anymore. I exchanged a great burden for tremendous freedom when I left.

"I've got a job in Alaska." Ben's news came as a complete surprise.

"You're kidding me?!" I responded enthusiastically, though my heart contracted at the memory of our dream to live in Alaska together.

"No, really. I'll be moving up there at the end of the month." Excitement edged his voice.

"Wow."

"I'm having a hard time believing it myself, ya' know?"

"Yeah. Alaska is a really long way."

"Tye, I know we're divorced, and you are moving on with your life. I hope that you are really happy. That's what I want."

A frightening mix of emotions welled up in me at my ex-husband's words. I'd even been practicing the "ex" title for several months, trying to get used to it. Learning that he'd be going to Alaska without me brought another twist.

"Ben," I managed, "I want you to be happy, too. Congratulations."

I'd begun to see someone else, and Ben knew it. I met Greg at a restaurant, and we had formed a beautiful friendship. Greg was passionate about his faith. The main topic of our conversation was always what God was doing in our lives or what we were learning from the Bible. We enjoyed each other's company and always tried to put God first.

After dating for several weeks, Greg proposed, and I said yes.

Ironically, Ben and I began to talk on the phone more frequently once he moved to Alaska. Our conversation moved from talking about the children, to his descriptions of his new surroundings, to both of us sharing more openly about our feelings and our faith. The communication grew deeper and richer than we had experienced in the months of separation.

"Uh … I guess that means the girls will have to come up for a visit?" I suggested, knowing they were eager to see their dad.

Ben paused, and then I heard familiar words. "Tye, you know that you are always welcome, too. I still love you with all of my heart. Whenever you are ready to come home, I'll be here."

I always found those words strangely comforting. His voice was strong, not pleading, as he reconfirmed his unconditional love to me every time we talked. Wherever he was, he always invited me to "come home," whether I had ever lived there or not.

But it was more than I deserved. I didn't know what to do with it.

"Good night, Ben." I closed the conversation and hung up.

Greg and I went out for dinner to talk about setting a date and planning the wedding. The conversation drifted, though, and we laughed that nothing was decided. Our next few dates went the same way. Finally, we sat quietly across the table from each other about two months after the proposal.

"I love you," Greg spoke first. Butterflies took flight in my stomach. His statement sounded unfinished, and I only nodded slightly for him to continue.

"I do love you, but I love you dearly as a friend," he said.

A sense of peace captured the butterflies ever so carefully and, after bringing them to rest, spread up into my heart. I took a deep breath and with relief stated, "I think that you are right."

We talked for a few minutes about the relationship and what we believed God wanted for each of us. Then he looked directly into my face. "Tye, I really think that you need to go back to Ben."

Confirmation — oddly, the word filled me with uncertainty. I opened the e-mail and reviewed three reservations on a one-way flight from Minneapolis to Anchorage. My heart became a pulsing wedge between my windpipe and my esophagus. "I can't do it. I just can't," I said to the computer monitor.

An hour later, I offered a pitiful refusal to Ben over the phone. "I'm so sorry. I just can't do it," I apologized. "I know that I told you I would, and I'm sorry that you already paid for the tickets. But I just can't do it."

Ben was quiet for a moment. When he spoke, I could hear disappointment in his voice. "That's okay, hon. I can't wait to see you. I miss you. But I don't want you to come unless you are ready."

I apologized again.

He answered with the same affirmation he'd given me every time we'd talked in the last 18 months. He still loved me and forgave me.

We talked about the children and where they'd be going when the school year began in just four weeks.

I sat silently for several minutes after we hung up. I pictured Ben in my mind, and my heart ached as much for my ex-husband as it did for me. In my mind's eye, I couldn't see myself with anyone else ever. At the same time, I had walked away and closed the door on the relationship. I separated and divorced Ben Zaleski.

For the next couple of weeks, I teetered between regret and relief that the girls and I were not moving to Alaska. They were disappointed, but like their dad, they maintained their support of my desire.

I pondered and prayed about everything that I had gone through, what I'd learned about God and about myself. I asked again for God to help me know his will. I considered that God had closed the book on another relationship, and that man had encouraged me to return to my first husband.

Finally, I determined that I was ready. Ben purchased tickets. I packed our things and prepared for the movers. He helped me make arrangements, and my car was picked up to be shipped to Alaska to arrive when we did.

Then, just days before we were to leave, I panicked. I lay awake at night with the paralyzing question, *What if I end up just as unhappy as before?*

The thought of getting on the airplane to fly a zillion miles away to a place that I'd never seen and being entrapped in the same unhappiness and depression I'd felt before was unbearable.

I sat my daughters down again and broke the news. "We're not going after all."

The looks on their faces told me that I'd better not do this to them again.

When I changed my mind a third time, Ben questioned me, "What are you afraid of?"

"I don't know," I answered with as much honesty as I thought I could.

"Are you afraid of me?" he asked.

"No," I sighed.

"The marriage?"

I couldn't answer.

"Or are you afraid of Alaska?"

I hung up the phone and knelt down to pray. "Lord, what am I afraid of?"

LOST

The girls just stared at me. I couldn't blame them for distrusting me. After all, this was the third time I had told them, "We're moving to Alaska to be closer to your dad."

We were on the plane, taxiing down the runway and into the air before they both turned to me with big smiles on their faces. My heart was pounding, but I smiled back. My spirit was completely at peace with my decision. I was following the Lord, and I knew it.

On that mild afternoon in October, the girls and I stepped out of the airplane at the top of the stairway leading down to the tarmac at Anchorage International Airport. Ben was waiting just outside the door of the terminal. Gabrielle ran toward his open arms. Jillian followed. My breath caught as I saw the man I'd been married to for 20 years and separated from for 18 months. He wrapped both girls up at the same time, hugging them and burying his head between theirs. Still holding them, he lifted his head and surveyed the approach. I was just near enough to make out his words, "Where's your mom?"

At that moment I caught his eye. I'd lost more than 100 pounds since we'd seen each other. I had lost far more in emotional baggage. God had done so much healing and transformation in my person that it changed my appearance. I was no longer weighted with the pain I'd carried since I was a child. Ben barely recognized me. Instantly, though, he brightened and covered the gap between us. Then he embraced me and whispered, "I'm so glad you are here."

THE DANCE PARTNER

Ben proudly introduced us to Anchorage and vice versa. But in our first moments with just the two of us, he said, "I can't wait to take you to the church I found here. You are going to love it."

I believed him.

Less than a month later, Alan flew in from college for the holidays. For the first Thanksgiving in two years, all five of us gathered around the dining table at Ben's place, reviving family traditions. One at a time, we took turns sharing words of thanksgiving for the blessings of the year. I was amazed at how all of my children had weathered the storms of the previous two years and come out strong and mature in their faith.

Ben waited to be the last to share. The children grew especially quiet, and we all turned to see him preparing to say something. He took a deep breath as he laid his napkin down and pushed his chair back slightly from the table. "I'm so thankful…" his voice broke. Pressing his right fist against his mouth, he cleared his throat.

"I am so thankful," he began, "that you are … that your mom is … here for Thanksgiving. God knows that there is nothing in the world that means more to me."

Out of the corner of my eye, I noticed the kids were getting teary-eyed. They'd taken hold of each other's hands like we used to do when we prayed together at dinnertime. Ben reached out and took my hands in his. I watched in amazement as he dropped down to one knee in front of me.

"I love you, Tye. Will you marry me?"

LOST

༈༈༈

God asks this question, "May I have this dance?" He doesn't make us do what we don't want to do. He is not manipulative and doesn't jerk us around or force us to do his will.

Yet that is what I expected of him at one time. My decisions as a child growing up had never been my own, and I felt comfortable asking God to just take care of me and make me do the right thing, or at least prevent me from doing the wrong thing.

When I became so unhappy with myself, I mistakenly blamed the marriage. The enemy of my heart had deceived me and made me think I was all alone.

I'd always been aware of God, as if he stood at the edge of the dance floor of my life. But I was dancing solo. I felt unworthy of his closeness, of his touch. I even felt unworthy of the earthly partner that he had given me.

But the Lord stood patiently there to the side; Ben did, too, while I stumbled about asking God to shout out the steps of the dance for my life. I strained to hear him and struggled to get in sync with him.

His loving invitation was to partner with him, and finally I had accepted his invitation. I allowed him to draw me into his arms where I came close enough to hear him whisper into my ear, "I love you. I forgive you. Now, follow me."

I surrendered to his lead, and the dance was becoming more graceful and effortless.

"Yes, yes, I will marry you." All five of us were laughing and crying at the same time.

In our dream come true, Ben and I were married six weeks later on January 6, 2007, on the upper floor of the Anchorage Hilton. The view of the mountains and the water and the snow were all as we had imagined Alaska would be. Our relationship with each other and with the Lord is even greater than I had ever imagined it could be.

Most of my life I lived in two spheres — my real life in which I moved on autopilot in sad, repetitive circles and the world of dance, where I fantasized my escape from the mundane. I was easily deceived by an enemy that was out to destroy me. Satan pushed me from one extreme to the other using fear and discontent. He provided just enough truth to obscure his lies. When I realized that I was wrong to leave my husband, that the source of my unhappiness was not the marriage but lack of relationship with God through Jesus Christ, I was ashamed. I had followed Christ for many, many years. I had gone to church faithfully and served with a number of ministries. Yet I wasn't close enough to realize I'd gotten lost in trying to escape the unhappiness. I wandered off the path.

"If we confess our sins, he is faithful and just and will forgive us our sins and purify us from all unrighteousness" (1 John 1:9).

Ben modeled Christ's forgiveness to me. I sensed the gentleness of the Lord Jesus leading me back, not just to the marriage, but to a completely surrendered relationship with the Lord.

LOST

My world is no longer divided in two, with a real world that is harsh and a separate world where dance is my escape. Instead, I'm living my life with true happiness from the inside out. The music and the dance are continuous and genuine, flowing from a heart that is loved and loves in return. I go to church because I want to, not because it is expected. I sing on the worship team at church because Jesus is my Savior. I love because he loved me first. I forgive because he has forgiven me. My life is the synchronized dance that the Lord has always intended it to be. Jesus is the music. Jesus is my partner. Jesus is the grace and the control in my every movement. Surrendered to him, my life is a dance of true freedom and happiness.

OUT OF THE WILD

THE STORY OF JOHN MARDEN
WRITTEN BY MARTY MINCHIN

We have been gone from the house for less than five minutes, books packed up for school, waiting at the bus stop. Mom sticks her head out of the front door. "Hey, boys," she bellows. Our heads turn in unison. Mom usually is too busy getting ready for her day to say much to us in the morning. "You're not going to school today!"

We are wild kids, my brothers and I. We skip school all of the time, wiling away afternoons at the arcade or roaming around our neighborhood on the outskirts of Detroit. A day out of seventh grade with my mother's permission? Cool.

Roger and I traipse back to the house, a hop in our step as we dream up big plans for a day of playing hooky. This might be a great day to throw snowballs at cars speeding down I-75, or we could grab some friends and catch rides on car bumpers. I smile at the thought of the mischief we can get into and bounce through the front door into the house.

Three dark-colored suitcases lined up in the living room stop me in my tracks. A few minutes earlier, when we had left for school, it had just been a nice, clean area.

"What's with them?" I ask, pointing at the row of dark-colored bags.

LOST

Mom silently faces us, her face serious. Our stepdad is upstairs, leaving her to deal with this problem on her own. We line up in front of her, staring at our feet and waiting for what can't be good news.

"You're going to live with your dad in Alaska," Mom replies in an even tone, like she's telling us she's going to the grocery store. "We're leaving for the airport in 15 minutes."

"Who?" I ask. My stomach drops as I process what she's saying. "Are you kidding? We haven't seen Pops in six years."

There is no time to run, no time to rebel. Mom has us cornered in the living room, and she's already packed our bags for Alaska. The three suitcases are for Roger, Bruce and me. Our brother Glen, for some reason, gets to stay.

❧❧❧

My first real memory of my dad was from around 1970. I am about 5 years old, the youngest of eight children born within a 12-year span. Pops had taken off about a year before, saying he had never wanted all of these kids. He said he wanted a different life, and it didn't involve my five brothers, two sisters and me.

Pops calls out of the blue one day. He's visiting our town in Michigan, and he wants the kids to meet him at the park. A fleeting feeling of happiness overcomes me. *My dad is here! He wants to see us!*

We play at the park for a few hours, goofing around

and climbing on the playground equipment. Pops builds a campfire for us to grill some hotdogs for dinner, and we gather around the small fire like we're waiting for Pops to revel us with ghost stories. It almost feels normal, like we're a happy bunch of kids just hanging out with our dad. Suddenly, Pops stands up, walks over to his truck and pulls a gleaming green 5-speed Schwinn bicycle out of the back. Instead of gears, it has a stick shift on the middle bar. You don't see bicycles like this in our neighborhood much.

He slowly wheels the bicycle toward the four of us circled around the fire, and we stare in anticipation like it's Christmas morning and we've caught Santa bringing in the gifts. My heart is pounding, hoping that he'll push the bike right over to me.

"Roger, come here," Pops says as he parks the beautiful bike in front of us, the afternoon sun glinting off the shiny paint. "This is for you. Happy birthday, son."

I stare at my feet. The excited beating in my chest changes to a crushing feeling as I realize the bicycle isn't for all of us to share or just for me. I glance up. Maybe Pops will walk back to the truck and get another bike out! But he just stands there, arms crossed over his puffed-out chest, watching proudly as Roger runs his hands over the brand-new handlebars.

"Wow. Thanks, Pops!" Roger says. The rest of us glare at him with pure envy.

Roger hops on the Schwinn and takes the bike for a test ride. He's right in front of us, feeding our anger and disappointment as he rides his bike, and we stand there with nothing. "Roger," I call as he loops back in front of us. I wave my hands wildly to get his attention. "Let me have a try!"

"No way!" Roger replies, pushing off for another trip around the park. Pops beams, so proud of the expensive present he's given my brother. The rest of us might as well have been invisible.

I know now how Joseph's brothers must have felt when he got that coat of many colors. He really scored, and the brothers had to watch silently while his father bestowed an amazing gift on him.

My heart is broken. To see that kind of extravagance out of my Pops, a man so stingy he couldn't even give me a few minutes of his time for a phone call after he left, is highly unusual. *Pops has been gone for a year. Why didn't he bring me a present, even something small? What did the rest of us do that was so bad?*

బాబాబా

Pops drives us back to the house that evening and walks us in the door. Something trips in him when he catches sight of Mom's live-in boyfriend, a tall, mean Vietnam veteran who is fresh out of the war. Mom has always been a sucker for a man in a uniform.

"Who are you?" Pops yells, his stocky frame tensing up. "What are you doing in this house?"

The boyfriend's face turns pale, like he's been caught

with his hand in a big cookie jar, but he isn't one to back down. He steps toward Pops. "I live here now."

My brothers and I cower against the wall. The intricacies of a broken marriage, a new boyfriend and an estranged, angry husband are too complicated to comprehend. All I know is they are cussing, screaming; there's a 16-gauge shotgun; someone grabs Mom, and the men are about to throw punches.

"If you don't get out of this house right now, I'm calling the cops," Mom's boyfriend growls.

Pops lowers the gun. He's already been in trouble with the law, and these are the magic words. Pops slinks out the door, hardly giving his frightened kids another look.

He's in town for a few days, staying at a motel, but we don't see him again for another six years.

ॐॐॐ

Mom marries and divorces the Vietnam veteran, then marries a guy who says he loves her, loves us and loves our life. He wants to live in Detroit, so we pack up and move to a duplex-style house outside the city. My stepdad has a job painting cars.

As soon as they get married, this man makes it clear that he's only interested in Mom. I guess eight children are too much for him, too. You can tell he doesn't like us. Mom chooses to work on her nursing career and go to night school. She's never home, never around to be our mother.

LOST

My brothers and I aren't supervised, so we skip school, earn a few dollars here and there mowing lawns and spend the money at the arcade where we can hang out with the older kids. In the winter, we drag discarded Christmas trees around the neighborhood and set them on fire. Sometimes a bunch of us grab on to the rear bumpers of vehicles and hitch rides around the neighborhood. If we can get enough kids on one car, we can bring it to a stop with our weight.

One night about 8, Mom says she and my stepdad have something to tell the four of us boys who are still living at home. We gather around her in the living room. Mom rarely has conversations with us, much less anything important to tell us.

"We're taking a vacation to Florida," she announces. "And we're leaving tomorrow morning." By "we," she means *her* and *my stepdad.* There's no discussion of this startling news.

I am about 9 years old, and her words don't seem real. It's time for bed, anyway, because we have school the next day. I walk to the bedroom I share with Roger and give little thought to the vacation. I'm asleep soon after my head hits the pillow.

The next day, Roger, Bruce, Glen and I get out of bed like we do every morning and head for the kitchen. It's time for breakfast, and we need to get ready for school. We always eat in the upstairs kitchen in our duplex, and a short hallway leads from our room to the entrance to the upstairs living area, where Mom and my stepdad also stay.

OUT OF THE WILD

I grab the doorknob and turn, and my hand abruptly stops.

"Mom?" I yell at the locked door, pressing my ear to the door to listen for any sounds of movement on the other side. "Are you in there? Hello? Mom?"

Silence. I bang on the door. They must have overslept.

"Where are you, Mom? Why is the door locked? Mom?"

Roger and I look at each other. They really have gone to Florida, and they've locked us out of half the house. I wish I could say we were surprised, but so many bad things had happened to us that this just seemed like one more episode we had to figure out how to handle.

"The other door," we blurt out at the same time. There's another door through an outside porch that leads upstairs, and we trot outside to try it. *Maybe they left that one unlocked for us. I bet it's open.* I grab the handle, but it won't turn. It's locked, too. Our last hope is the downstairs refrigerator, but when I open the door, only the bare light stares back at me. All of the food is locked upstairs. Our stomachs are rumbling for breakfast now, and we begin to panic. I slowly close the door to the empty refrigerator, and I can tell Roger is thinking the same thing I am: We have to get something to eat.

The problem is that I've never even bought milk before. Mom always keeps food in the refrigerator for us, and I never give a thought to where the food comes from or how it gets into the refrigerator. I have no money, no way to even buy food if I knew how to do it. My two

LOST

brothers and I, each of us a stepping stone apart in age, huddle together. We have to make a plan.

"Let's call Bruce," Glen suggests as Roger and I nod. "He'll bring us something to eat."

Bruce has already left for work at McDonald's, and when we call, he says he'll bring us a case of danishes that they'd otherwise throw out at the end of the shift. We'll have to make them last for a week.

I shove my books in my backpack and trudge to the bus stop, my stomach empty and grumbling.

Why, Mom? Why did you have all of these kids if you didn't want us? What did I do wrong? How could you just leave us with nothing?

❧❧❧

I don't even get to say goodbye to my brother Glen before Mom and her husband load Bruce, Roger and me into the backseat of her car for the drive to the Detroit airport.

I press my face against the car window, my mind going through all of the days at the arcade, all the mornings I decided not to go to school, all of the trouble I've gotten into. *Maybe if I had been better, Mom would still want me.*

The large glass doors slide open, and we walk silently into the airport. Nobody says much as we check in those suitcases and head to the gate. There, we meet the crisply dressed stewardess who will babysit us on the flight. It's time for Mom to go, and I can scarcely register that instead of sitting in my classroom today, I'm about to board a plane for Alaska. Mom reaches out to hug and kiss us goodbye. I step back from her.

Are you kidding? You're giving us the boot, and you expect us to hug you? Yeah, right.

We walk away from her; no goodbyes. I'm sure she is standing there watching her three sons leave, but we don't look back to find out.

The plane ride takes nine hours. Roger, Bruce and I goof around, watching movies and playing with the ashtrays, being told by the stewardess to behave every so often. An unexpected, strange excitement begins to grow in me, like maybe a new adventure is unfolding, and maybe Pops will be happy to see us.

The stewardess walks Roger, Bruce and me down the jet way and off the plane at the Anchorage airport. I scan the crowd, seeing face after face I don't recognize. I haven't laid eyes on Pops in six years, and I have no idea what he looks like.

Finally, a short, solid man strides toward us, scowling at the stewardess who is ready to hand over her three charges. *A flicker of recognition.* It's him, and I can tell he's not happy to see us.

I wonder if he was praying that the plane would crash?

We stand in a little circle at the gate, Pops and three of his sons. Awkwardly, we reach out our arms, too unfamiliar for an *"I missed you"* or a one-on-one embrace. We do a little group hug, then quickly recoil and fall into step behind Pops, striding toward our new life.

It's March of 1978, and the temperature in Anchorage is below 20 degrees. Pops leads us to his 1976 Datsun pickup in the airport parking lot. The bed of the truck is piled high with 25 cases of bread. Pops would never miss a chance to pick up some food for his sled dogs. The cases are crammed in, stacked almost as high as the top of the truck.

I'm the youngest at 12 years old, so I get the seat of honor in the cab. Pops shoves the suitcases in with the bread, shifting the crates around to make room.

"Get in there," he grumps, motioning Roger and Bruce into the back of the pickup. "And try not to mess up the bread too much."

The truck bumps and rumbles over 45 miles of Alaska roads, driving farther and farther into the wilderness. My stomach contracts and sinks with each jolt.

Where are we going? I thought Pops said this was a short drive.

We finally pull up in front of a little log cabin like you'd see in a school history book. It's covered with snow, and the branches of the evergreens around it hang low from the heavy snow piled on them. Pops' sled dogs bark and pull at their chains as we approach the cabin. We're so tired from the flight that we don't even open our bags. We barely say hello to Pops' wife and fall asleep wherever we can find a spot on the floor.

"Time to get up!" Pops calls the next morning, waking us from a jetlag slumber. We hardly have time to remember where we are before he's motioning us toward a door. "Grab your bags, boys, and I'll show you where you're going to stay."

We dutifully pick up the three suitcases, which Mom had somehow packed with clothes without us knowing. I have wondered where our bedroom in the cabin will be, but Pops opens the door and leads us into the freezing outside air. He motions to a camper parked about 50 feet from the cabin, which, like us, looks like an afterthought to his life.

"You all are going to stay out here," he says. "Look, there's an overhead bed, and a table folds down, and you'll each have a bunk."

He's trying to make this lonely little camper sound like a cool place to hang out, but I know what it really is: a place as far away from he and his wife as he can find. At least at Mom's we got to live in the house. This is a whole new reality.

We squeeze into the camper to check out our new lodgings, feeling like a bunch of stray dogs that aren't welcome in the house with the family. I seethe with anger at my mom. She doesn't want us, and she sent us to live with a man who doesn't want us, either. I never write her a letter, never call her. She has betrayed us.

❧❧❧

Pops works us like little slaves. Every day we tramp from our camper to the cabin, where we get a bland

LOST

breakfast of corn mush or oatmeal before school. We only have a propane heater in the camper, so we spend as little time in there as possible.

After school, Pops sends us right out into the forest for more wood, and we often chop until after dark, swinging the ax over and over until our arms ache and freeze. The dogs come along, dragging the sled that will carry the wood back to the cabin.

We eventually move into the cabin after a mattress leaning against the camper catches fire and burns down our shelter. But Pops makes us build an addition onto his cabin first so there will be enough room for all of us. We have no electricity or running water, so we keep chopping wood to maintain a fire in the stove and provide some warmth against the freezing Alaska weather.

Pops is a hard man to be around. He doesn't like kids, and he doesn't like jokes and roughhousing. We never play little league or basketball or high school sports. We just work. There are times we imagine he loves us. One day, I try to give him a hug.

I reach out, move toward him. I hold out my young boy's arms and touch the material of Pops' shirt. For a moment, he lifts his arms, and they close around me.

Then he realizes what he's doing. He steps away like he's touched a hot coal, backpedaling from any show of affection.

You're all I have, Pops. Mom doesn't want Roger, Bruce or me, and there's nobody else. Why am I such a disappointment to you?

OUT OF THE WILD

࿄࿄࿄

We wait for Sunday mornings like the first day of summer vacation. Sometimes we hang around with the neighbor kids on the next property over, and they go to church every week. On Sundays, we pack into their pickup truck, driving into a blissful few hours away from Pops and chores. He glares as we scamper away. Pops is an atheist; God is for weak people.

Church feels wonderful and free. I happily sit in Sunday school and the service soaking up Bible teaching and worship.

God sounds great, but I don't see much hope for myself. My family is broken; my parents don't want me. Where in the world does God fit into that?

࿄࿄࿄

"How was school today?" Pops asks me one afternoon as we come in the door, fishing around to see if we'd actually attended school. "Was it all right?"

"Yeah," I reply, tossing down my book bag.

Something snaps inside Pops, like a twig stepped on in the woods. His raging voice breaks the eerie silence.

"You answer me, 'Yes' or 'Yes, sir'!" His face is red; his eyes are wide and crazy. He strides toward me, arms raised like a fighter, and he smacks me on the cheek with one hand, across the other cheek with the other hand.

Bang, bang, bang. He's raging, shoving me, and I cover my face from the blows.

LOST

"Pops, what did I do?" I cower, retreating toward the wall. "Why are you so mad?"

I hunch over and scoot backward, then spring forward in surprise when my back touches the red-hot stove, my hand burning where I'd grabbed it by accident. Thankfully, Pops backs off when he sees how hurt I am. For today, the beating is over.

This isn't the first time we've seen Pops' violent side. One time he didn't like that I borrowed a cup of sugar from a neighbor, so he buried a spruce pole in the ground, tied me to it and whipped me with a bull whip. I'd never even seen him beat his sled dogs like that.

"We can't live here," Roger whispers to me that night as I tend to my burns. "Bro, there's got to be a better life than this." I've been growing closer to God, and I have already told him I can't stay with Pops anymore. Roger's statement is just an affirmation of what I already know.

"We'll leave tomorrow for school and never come back," I tell my brother. As soon as Bruce had saved up and bought a pickup truck, Pops had told him to drive himself away and never come back. Now he would be free of his other two sons.

☙☙☙

Roger and I stay with unwitting friends as long as we can and then enter the foster-care system, bouncing around between families until we graduate from high school.

OUT OF THE WILD

I start smoking pot, seriously, soon after leaving Pops' house. At this time pot is legal in Alaska, and it's easy to smoke with friends from school. I am developing a bad attitude, and I need to escape. Pot is an easy answer, and it's easy to find. Many people around here grow it.

One of my foster families goes to church, and I go with them. I keep in contact with God, and after high school, I decide that if I have made it through the beatings and living with parents who didn't want me, God must really be with me. If there's anyone he can offer protection to, it's me.

So one Sunday, I invite God into my heart.

But I wonder, *Does God really love me? Did he really forgive me for whatever I had done that made my parents not want me? Am I worthy of anyone's love, much less God's?*

God and I begin a dance. I take two steps forward with him, and Satan pulls me a few steps back. Sometimes God and I are close, but I am slowly moving toward disaster.

৵৵৵

The phone rings one afternoon in 2003 when I'm at work. It's my mother.

"John, I've got bad news," she says. "Your brother Dave died."

I know it has to be a car crash because that is the logical thing. Dave's hobby is car racing, and he likes to race drag cars. He's a high-speed kind of guy.

LOST

Mom keeps talking. My heart sinks.

"He shot himself in the chest and killed himself."

Four years ago, I had received the same phone call about my brother Glen, the one who Mom allowed to stay in Detroit while she shipped Bruce, Roger and me to Alaska. Glen drove out on a lonely road in Colorado and shot himself. I wish he had called me or any of our siblings first. We may have been separated as kids, but we were still a family. Whatever bad day Glen was having, I could have talked to him about it and prayed with him. I wonder if he felt just like we did, questioning why Mom made him stay in Detroit rather than sending him with us to live with Pops.

Now, another brother, another suicide…

I have always looked up to Dave. When we were kids, he would wrestle all four of us little boys and take us easily. One of my best family memories is when my brothers came to Alaska for Pops' funeral, and I took Dave, Glen and their wives down a trail on snow machines. We rode the curving snow trails through the tall trees, slowing at one point as we passed through a herd of moose. I loved the feeling of brotherhood and showing them God's amazing creation in my part of the world.

I slowly walk to my office at the power plant and close the door. The silence helps me absorb the words I have just heard, the sense of loss that washes over me. Another brother has killed himself. How can this be?

Then I start screaming at the wall, at the desk, at any place where God might listen.

OUT OF THE WILD

God, why did you let this happen? I can't believe you would let him kill himself. Dave had a good life. Why would he do this?

Thoughts of other close friends who had died fill my mind. Death is unfair, whether it is my brothers killing themselves or a good friend, a survivor of the battle of Mogadishu, who senselessly died in a car crash.

Taking a deep breath, I open my office door. I have to get myself under control long enough to walk to my truck and drive away. I quietly tell my boss I am leaving, and I get into my truck for the long ride home.

The first store that sells whiskey beckons to me like a star in the swirl of anger, disbelief and loss in my head. I pull into the parking lot and buy a bottle of whiskey. As soon as I get back on the road, I let the tears run down my face, and I take deep swigs from the bottle. I have a bag of weed on me, so I smoke some pot, waiting for the drugs and alcohol to make me numb.

Angie, my wife, knows something is wrong when I walk in the door with the neck of the whiskey bottle clutched in my hand. She is right. My mental breakdown has begun.

ॐॐॐ

That summer and fall, I spend $10,000 drinking myself into oblivion. I take four bottles of whiskey with me to work a seven-day shift. For three or four years, I am drunk every waking moment.

LOST

I am an angry man. I get mad a lot, and I quit jobs in a second if I don't like the way the boss looks at me. I just pick up my tools and walk off the job site. Once, I leave a job that pays $35 an hour, and there are many days I wish I had that one back.

I lose years of my life, passing the days drunk and stoned. I am married and have children, and amazingly my wife stays with me. We go to church at Church on the Rock almost every Sunday, but I refuse to put my trust in God. I am drowning in guilt and drowning my feelings with drugs and alcohol.

Sometimes people tell me they worked with me during those years, and I can't remember ever meeting them.

༅༅༅

My daughter steps out of her bedroom and lets out a bloodcurdling scream that shakes me out of 10 years of stupor.

That scream travels from my brain to my toes, an unearthly sound like nothing I've ever heard. I'm on my way outside to kill myself. I move my hand off the trigger, lower the gun from my head and turn to StephAnnie, a young teenager standing there in her Sunday dress, her eyes wide open, screaming like a girl in a horror movie.

StephAnnie and I are close, and I can read her face. *Daddy, why would you do this? I adore you. Do you think so little of me that you would do this to yourself?*

I hear God in my head. *I'm not ready for you to kill*

yourself. I have something better for you. Don't get stupid. You need to be sober and straight.

Angie runs up the stairs, the pounding of her feet muffled by StephAnnie's screams. I hadn't wanted to go to church that morning, feeling the heavy funk that comes over me early in the year when my brothers' and Pops' birthdays and death days came around. I'm angry, drunk and high, and I told Angie that morning, like I have many times before, that I'd be better off dead … that I might as well go be with my brothers. It's been three years since Dave killed himself, and I miss him.

I lay the 40-caliber handgun on a table. Angie and StephAnnie are silent. *Wow, I can't believe I did that.*

❧❧❧

The next Sunday, I walk forward at church and ask for prayer. I was a blubbering, self-pitying drunk, and I had almost killed myself. I need God's intervention.

There are a lot of deaths racked up in my family, God. Suicide is overwhelming me. This is a curse that needs to be broken.

I feel a warm comfort envelop me, like God is giving me a hug.

I understand the pain you're going through, my child. I've got you covered. Thank you for admitting what's really getting to you right now.

❧❧❧

LOST

On a clear day in early 2009, I spend several days in Valdez waiting for a job that never comes through. There are few places in the world that are as beautiful as Valdez, and that day the sunshine on those majestic mountains takes my breath away.

I have some time on my hands, so I drive out to a glacier and park next to it, settling in for an afternoon with a bag of weed. I relax in the driver's seat, content to enjoy the view out the window, get stoned and commune with God. I have smoked pot for more than 20 years, and I am pretty sure that God doesn't really care if I'm stoned when I talk to him. At least I'm talking to him at all.

This day, in God's amazing timing, he catches me in a rare sober moment.

I think about how I'd heard God say a few years before that I need to stop smoking pot. I have told Angie that if I ever have to choose between pot and work, I'll choose work. I've managed large teams of people and done very well at my job, all while I was smoking, but these days jobs do random drug testing, which I'll certainly fail.

I've been trying to wean myself off pot for several years, but I keep fighting it. I honestly can't envision myself not smoking pot, and I've even joked with Angie that if I die, she should toss some weed in my casket, just in case.

Even though, my relationship with God is growing strong. I have been going to church a lot more, and my belief is overwhelming me. The love I feel for God is so much more than when I was a teenager. Then, I knew that

I was a child of God — that he was there and existed. Now, I am living for God like I am supposed to. I'm sure now that God will forgive me for smoking pot. It's time to put this down.

I have something for you, I hear God say, *but you can't be like this.*

I know the time to make a change is right now.

Lord, I'm finally ready to submit. I'm going to commit to stop smoking pot if you keep your word that you will not give me anything more than I can handle. I'm going to trust in your word. I know that Satan has his strongest grip on me when I'm smoking pot.

I slowly smoke the rest of the pot in the bag, then I break the pipe I smoked it with.

Ten days later, I give Angie the greatest Valentine's gift I have: me, free from pot. After all of these years of her worrying about me, I am going to show her some real change and true love by quitting something she has asked me to stop for years.

That day, God works a miracle. I never smoke pot again.

ॐॐॐ

A few months later, my older sister Cathy calls.

"We've found Bruce," she says. I kind of know what she means, but I don't want to believe it. So I joke.

"I didn't know he was lost."

Cathy doesn't laugh.

LOST

"We found him dead in the back of his work truck, John. He killed himself."

The last time I saw Bruce I had been helping him out with his asbestos abatement business in a nearby town. He had suffered a terrible motorcycle accident, and he could hardly lift an empty bag over his head, so I helped with the manual labor. He often sat and watched, and I could tell he was frustrated that he couldn't do the work himself anymore.

He had started seeing a gal, and his wife had left him. I tried to tell him that what he was doing wasn't right, but he didn't want to hear any preaching from me. "I'll ask forgiveness for everything at one time," he would say. "I'm not through sinning yet." I didn't get his real meaning at the time. I thought the Lord might be working in his heart and that he might one day turn around and ask for forgiveness and repent.

Cathy tells me they found him dead in the back of his work truck, where he had asphyxiated himself.

I shed some tears, but not the torrent I'd cried after Dave committed suicide. I don't yell, scream or get mad at God. Instead, I tell Cathy I'll come see her, and I spend some time with Mom. She is hurting. Her dad killed himself by stepping in front of a train, and now three of her six sons have committed suicide, too.

I can't get mad, because I've already tried it. I can't smoke my way out of this, I can't drink my way out of this. I didn't handle it right when Glen and Dave killed themselves.

I cling to I Corinthians 10:13: "No temptation has overtaken you except what is common to mankind. And God is faithful; he will not let you be tempted beyond what you can bear. But when you are tempted, he will also provide a way out so that you can endure it."

Lord, I want your healing power. Three of my brothers are dead, and you're giving me a lot.

God is shaping and molding me, all for a purpose. I can feel it working, because this time, with the devastating news of yet another brother's suicide, I'm not hurting as much.

"Hey, boss," I call out. I've waited for the right time to ask him for some time off. "I need five days to go to Seldovia to talk about suicide prevention."

He turns and looks at me like I'm crazy, not for asking for vacation time, but for talking about suicide.

"Why would you do that?"

You don't have a clue. If three of your brothers had killed themselves, maybe you'd have to finally stand up and say something, too.

I get the vacation days and take a van ride and a ferry to Seldovia with a team from Carry the Cure, a group that goes out to Alaskan villages and talks to people about suicide prevention. Some of the villages are so remote that you can only reach them in a small aircraft. The isolation leads to drinking, depression and domestic violence, and children and adults end up committing suicide or cutting themselves to deal with it.

We meet with 30 or 40 teenagers from the village, and one night after our concert, God nudges me to look toward a teenage girl standing with her friends. She's clearly popular, dressed in black pants and a white shirt and chatting with the other teenagers. The leader asks the group to repeat after him a vow of life, and I watch this girl. As the other kids around her are saying the vow, she doesn't even bother to mouth it. I'm caught off guard.

Go talk to her, God tells me. *She needs to hear your message.*

After a few minutes, I walk over to one of the local group leaders. "What's the deal with this gal right over there?" I ask. "Is she okay?"

"Her name's Rebecca," the gal replies, following my glance. "She's one of the people you guys came down here for."

I am bold with God's affirmation of my gut feeling about this girl. As I walk toward her with one of my team members, I can see the inch-high scar tissue on her wrist. It's wide and the length of her wrist, like a morbid bracelet symbolizing her desire to die. Many people who cut themselves make small incisions; it's obvious something terrible is making Rebecca hurt herself so badly.

"Hi," I say. "Did you enjoy the concert?"

"It was okay."

Clearly, Rebecca doesn't want to talk. She's friendly enough, but she's standing behind a brick wall.

OUT OF THE WILD

༒ ༒ ༒

I sit by Rebecca in a class the next day. Bill, one of the leaders, is talking about bullying and suicide. He outlines the symptoms of people who may commit suicide, including cutting.

A girl's hand shoots up.

"If you know someone who cuts themselves, what should you do?" the girl asks Bill.

Rebecca whips her head around and glares at her. "You should mind your own business," she snaps at her friend. The girl sinks down into her seat.

Only a really good plastic surgeon could remove that scar tissue from Rebecca's wrist. It's the kind of scar that doesn't take a sunburn, that remains pale while the sun browns the skin around it.

Why would a young woman with such a promising future hurt herself so badly? Why won't she let anyone help her? What kind of pain is she going through?

Rebecca pulls out the journal we've given each teenager, and I notice that she's doodled all over the front. These aren't just girly scribbles of flowers and hearts. She's drawn cartoons, like Pokemon, and they're good. Maybe she's into art. Maybe I should send her some art supplies when I get home.

I hear God confirming my idea. *You're thinking it, and you need to go do it.*

I call my sister when I get home, and we drive right to the store. I send Rebecca a package of pencils, art paper and paint supplies with a letter giving her Angie and my phone number and telling her to call us if she ever needs to talk to someone who's not in her village. I try to give her some of the hope that God has given me.

A friend confirms that Rebecca received the package, but that's all I know.

&c&c&c

God has opened up opportunities for me to speak about suicide prevention in the last year. I tell people that suicide is a permanent solution to a temporary problem, and God is a permanent solution to a temporary problem. When my brothers had a bad day, they chose suicide.

But God will get you through whatever pain you're experiencing, and he has arms big enough to forgive anybody for anything.

My Christian life has begun to grow in amazing and unimaginable ways since that day I quit smoking pot. I know God has a purpose for my life, and today I can say that there is a loving God who cares about every individual and what he or she is going through.

My family has turned around 180 degrees, and my four remaining siblings and I are a small, tight group. Several of them have moved here to Alaska and live in my neighborhood.

I'm so thankful for Angie and her prayers and patience all of these years and that I've been here to watch my children grow up.

OUT OF THE WILD

I still think about suicide sometimes, but I know that Satan is putting those thoughts in my head. When I hear, *You can go be with your brothers,* I turn to God. My Christian brothers at Church on the Rock still pray for me, just like they did that day in 2007 when I almost killed myself. I'm sure God's looking down and saying, *After all you've been through, you're standing by me. Thanks, son.* It gives me a sense of joy, a sense of hope, and there is no reason I will ever need to consider putting a gun to my head again.

WALLS
THE STORY OF DANIEL SLOAN
WRITTEN BY KAREN KOCZWARA

This is not how I want to die.

The water was rising quickly. I had to get out of here, but my body was too weak to move, my head too clouded to think straight. Panic rose in my chest as I glanced around my dark prison. My Humvee, a machine of metal meant to protect me, had now become my worst enemy. And time was running out.

"You here, man?" I called to my buddy, but only silence answered. The 115 pounds of gear on my back felt like twice as much as I fought to stay above the water. It was hard to recall just what had happened; one minute, we'd been driving, the next, rolling off a cliff. Then there had been only blackness. It was surreal, the sort of nightmare I'd only heard about from my buddies. But there was no time to sort out the details; I had to get out of here before the water trapped me for good!

God, help me! I don't want to drown here! This is not how I want to die!

෯෯෯

Most of the time, walls are a good thing. Four walls can make up a home, the place where we sit around the dining table, tuck our kids in and say our prayers. Walls are meant to protect, shield the pain, keep the outside where it belongs. But sometimes, we build walls that aren't meant to be. Slowly, one brick at a time, they grow higher, until we don't have a clue how to tear them down.

As a child, my "four walls" changed quite a bit. I was born January 11, 1985, in Three Hills, Alberta, Canada, where my parents were attending Prairie Bible College. At the age of 2, I moved to a remote part of Nepal; my parents became missionaries with International Nepal Fellowship. We lived there until I was 6 and then moved to Washington. For a while, there was only my older brother, Jake, and me. When I was 7, my parents adopted my sister from Bulgaria, and our family was now complete.

From as far back as I could remember, my life revolved around church. My parents had both attended Bible school in Washington and felt led to pursue a life of ministry from then on. Thus, my early years were full of adventure as we watched my dad follow one "calling" after the next. In 1996, Dad had a big announcement for the family. We were moving to Talkeetna, Alaska, so they could start the Master's Commission, a Bible training program for young adults.

I was less than thrilled about the move. At the peak of adolescence, I had enough to worry about. I tried to "think of it as an adventure" as we loaded the moving boxes into the truck. Perhaps this time we'd settle down for good.

Talkeetna, home to the stunning Mount McKinley,

was a young boy's paradise. Kayaking, hiking and hunting were just a few ways to keep busy during the long summer days. I looked forward to exploring the rugged wilderness with my dad, but most days, he was too busy for fun. The Master's Commission began to eat up all of Dad's time, and soon I began to grow resentful.

"This is very important and exciting, Daniel," my mother tried telling me as she poked her head in my room to say goodnight. "Your father is really doing some great things with the program, developing potential church leaders and ministers. We must all be supportive."

I was thankful it was dark so she could not see my face twisted into a scowl. As the door closed, I leaned back on my pillow and sighed. *Supportive.* Hadn't we been just that since the day we were born? What about *our* family? What about me? This ministry stuff was all good, but didn't we come first?

When Sunday rolled around, I drug my feet into the church and tried not to roll my eyes as the pastor spoke. I'd heard the same Bible stories since I was a kid; did I really need to spend the rest of my life hearing about Noah's Ark? It was all beginning to seem a bit pointless.

One Sunday, however, a pretty girl walked into church and sat down next to her mother. After the service, I made a point to introduce myself.

"I'm Daniel," I said casually as we filed out of the pews. "I think our moms are friends."

"Katrina." Her eyes sparkled as she smiled. "You can call me Trina, though."

LOST

"Trina," I repeated, my throat suddenly going dry. "Okay. Nice to meet you."

Trina and I wrote notes back and forth for a couple months and then began spending time together. She was the first "girl" friend I'd ever had, and I enjoyed her company more than she knew. Though we were young, I felt myself falling for her. When we kissed for the first time, it felt like the real deal. At 15, I didn't know much, but I was certain of one thing: I couldn't imagine my life without Trina.

Things grew tenser at home. My father became more consumed with the Master's Commission, leaving little time for us to spend together. I grew angry not just at him, but at God. If ministry was supposed to be such a great thing, why was it taking such a toll on our family?

"Your dad loves you; you know that, right?" Trina whispered to me one winter night. We were standing outside a cabin at Byer's Lake during an overnight youth group trip. Trina had gotten saved and was excited about her new relationship with God. I was happy for her but still struggling with my own feelings about God.

I shrugged. I'd grown almost numb over the past few years; I was just tired of the whole church scene. It didn't seem worth it anymore. "I dunno," I mumbled. I slipped my hand into Trina's, thankful that I had her to lean on. These days, Trina was the only good thing in my life.

"*I like you*, Daniel," Trina added quietly.

I sucked in my breath. I knew Trina liked me, and I liked her, too, but saying it aloud was a whole other thing.

WALLS

"I *like* you," I replied, my heart soaring. Suddenly, the moment felt right; I leaned over and gently kissed her. The chill of the night was replaced by a warmth in my heart. My life might be worthless, but at least I had my girl.

Back at home, I still struggled to gain attention from my father. One night, overcome with a fresh wave of anger, I pulled my 22 (the rifle I used to shoot squirrels) out from under my bed. Without giving it much thought, I held it to my head and impulsively pulled the trigger. To my relief and simultaneous disappointment, the gun wasn't loaded. I threw it down and shoved it back under the bed. My hands shook as I pulled the covers over my head and tried to fall asleep. Stupid gun, stupid life. What was the point, anyway?

My destructive behavior continued as I tried to get my parents' attention. I drove recklessly, getting into four separate car accidents. I performed crazy jumps with my dirt bike and did back flips off 30-foot cliffs into the water. Perhaps if I kept acting out, they'd take notice and quit the ministry for a while to focus on me.

One afternoon, my mother pulled me aside and asked if we could go for a walk. As our feet crunched the gravel beneath us, she poured out her heart. "I really don't like the man you're becoming, Daniel," she said quietly. "I see this resentment, this anger built up in you, and I don't know where it comes from. It makes me so sad. Your dad and I have tried everything to show you we love you, but somehow, we just can't seem to get through." She took a deep breath and began to cry.

LOST

I kicked at the dirt and looked the other way. I loved my mother and hated to see her cry. I knew I'd hurt her, that her words were dead on. Still, I couldn't pretend all was fine. I was tired of being a pastor's kid, having all eyes on me and my family as we delved into one ministry "opportunity" after the next. I may be the black sheep of the family, but I needed to find my own pasture to roam in.

Not long after our talk, my parents pulled me aside again, concern vivid in their eyes. "Daniel, we don't know what else to do. We can see you're unhappy here in Alaska, and we thought it might be best if you went to stay with your aunt and uncle in Missouri for a while. You can get to know your cousins better and enjoy a change of scenery. What do you think?"

I didn't want to leave Trina, but I wasn't very keen on staying here anymore. And so, after promising Trina I'd write and call every day, I headed out to Missouri. My four walls would change once again. Missouri was like night and day to Alaska. I traded mountains for prairies and structure for freedom. To my surprise, it wasn't all bad. I enjoyed spending time with my cousins and was happy to be relieved of the pastor's kid label for a while. I missed Trina like crazy, however, and couldn't wait to be together with her again.

I returned to Alaska, but not long after, a pastoring job opened up for my father back in Camdenton, Missouri, and we moved once again. I was disappointed, as this meant I would most likely not see Trina much anymore.

WALLS

We still remained faithful to each other, writing letters and calling just as we'd promised. Trina always tried to encourage me over the phone.

"God's doing some good stuff in my life," she gushed one day. "I'm praying for you, too, Daniel."

I was happy for Trina, though I was not in the same place with her spiritually. I had put God on the back burner for now, trading church services for partying.

Still, if anyone could help me keep a level head, it was Trina. She always knew just what to say and never disappointed. I was thankful for her influence in my life, even if I could not allow my heart to match hers when it came to God.

On September 11, 2001, I watched along with the rest of the world as the Twin Towers in New York crumbled to the ground. As the military tanks rolled onto the scene, I sat up straight, my heart beating fast. I'd wanted to join the military since I was 12 years old; the minute I turned 18, I would find a way to sign up and serve my country.

When I was 17, my parents went on a month-long missions trip with Master's Commission; I stayed behind. One morning, a 23-year-old girl who was house sitting up the road let herself in my house and climbed into bed with me; I was taken aback at her boldness. Trina was the only girl in my life; we had saved ourselves for each other. Yet, Trina was thousands of miles away, while this attractive girl was just inches away from me. In a moment of weakness, I slept with her that night.

My secret gnawed away at me for weeks. One day, my

cousin came to me distressed. "Is it true, Daniel? You slept with my best friend?" she asked with wide eyes.

My heart sank. "Yes," I whispered. "It was stupid, so stupid."

"You have to tell Trina," she insisted.

"Oh, I can't. It's just gonna kill her," I moaned, putting my head in my hands. How stupid could I have been? Why couldn't I have just said no, resisted the temptation? Trina and I had a history, yet I'd destroyed it all in a heartbeat. The idea of telling her what I'd done made me physically sick.

At last, I worked up the guts to e-mail Trina. "I'm so, so very sorry," I wrote, my heart aching. "I hate myself for what I've done. I hate the person I've become." And I meant it. For the first time, I was able to see the selfish, destructive person I'd become. I hardly recognized myself when I looked in the mirror; where had the little boy who'd sung Bible songs and recited verses gone? I couldn't blame Trina a bit if she wanted nothing to do with me again.

To my utter devastation, Trina told me it was best if we broke up. "I don't think I can trust you after what you've done to me, Daniel," she cried. "You just ripped my heart in pieces."

Determined to turn my life around and become a better man, I began taking classes toward my diploma. I had paid little attention to my school work while homeschooling; if I wanted to join the military and make a life for myself, I'd have to step up my game.

WALLS

Within a few months, I began getting A's and B's on my papers and tests. My mother returned from a parent-teacher conference one day with a big smile on her face. "Your teachers had nothing but wonderful things to say about you!" she declared, beaming. "I'm so proud of you!"

Things were turning around for me on the outside, but on the inside, I was still a mess. I couldn't get over the fact that I'd let the love of my life down. And while I wanted to turn my heart back to God, I was still angry from years of emotional neglect. I began praying that he would show me a sign, that he would reveal himself to me in a big way. I thought of my father's goose bump-worthy testimony. He'd lived his life as an alcoholic and was headed nowhere fast when God literally turned his boat around. While on the water one day, his boat began to sink. He cried out for help, and God saved not just his body, but his soul. I didn't want to have to sink in the ocean for God to show up, but I did want to experience his presence in a real way.

After finishing my classes, I enlisted in the Marines on March 3, 2004. As I signed the contract, I couldn't help but think about Trina. Though we were not on speaking terms, I knew she would be terribly upset to learn I'd joined the military. I longed to reunite with her, but for now, I wanted to focus on serving my country. I wasn't certain about many things in my life, but joining the Marines was one thing I'd never doubted. I planned to give it my everything.

For me, boot camp was a joke. Having lived much of my life in Alaska, I'd done more physically grueling activities than most guys my age. While my peers grumbled, cried and moaned about pushups, I kept my cool. Boot camp was just the beginning, I knew. The real test would come when we deployed.

I began writing Trina letters, telling her how much I missed her and pleading with her to take me back. However, I didn't hear a word back. To fill the void, I began talking with a girl back in Missouri. My heart wasn't really in the relationship, but I needed someone to take my mind off the pain.

After boot camp, I went to infantry school at Camp Pendleton, California. Right away, I began to get noticed for my hard work and dedication. It felt great to be recognized for something other than goofing off or getting into trouble. When we got word we were headed to Haditha, Iraq, in August, I hardly flinched. It was a deployment, but I was more than ready to take it on.

Just before we left, I discovered my new girlfriend had been cheating on me. "That's it! I'm done with women! Forget them all!" I yelled angrily. But inside, my heart still beat for Trina. She was the only woman I wanted, the only one I'd *ever* wanted.

Nothing could have prepared me for the operation we were about to embark on in Haditha. These were early days in the Iraq war, and much had still to be accomplished here. Our leader explained to us that we'd be invading extremely hostile territory. Many lives had already been lost here; there was a chance we could lose ours, too. As a chaplain came and said a prayer over us, I looked around at the guys who'd become like brothers in such a short time. A few were already husbands and fathers; we were all too young to die. This was what we'd signed up for, though, and we would fight a good fight.

After being there nearly three weeks, we invaded the city. As I patrolled the outskirts of Haditha, I stood over the dam in the blazing heat, more than 100 pounds of gear fastened to my back, m16 strapped to my side, and my blood began to pump. Three huge rock piles lay to the left and right of me. Before I knew what was happening, rocks began to fly everywhere as the first shots were fired. I went down to the ground and rolled behind some rocks in a ditch. Bullets continued to fly over my head, one after another as insurgents fired on us. Within minutes, my life had become the scene of a suspense movie in which I could only pray ended in my favor.

My squad leader, a silver star recipient, fully took charge of the situation. He began firing back and barking orders, all the while keeping his cool. As I watched him demonstrate such bravery, the fire inside of me returned. Slowly, I stood up from behind the rocks and fired my gun. Each time I pulled the trigger, my heart pulsed faster. I'd claimed I was made for this moment; now it was time to step up to the plate!

The firing lasted for nearly two hours. Tanks rolled in and blew up several buildings we had taken fire from. We found and destroyed several road bombs, as well. When at last the fighting ceased, I set down my gun with trembling hands and took a deep breath. My feet felt like lead as we made our way back to the dam to sleep 36 hours later. We hardly spoke; our nerves were rattled, and we were exhausted. A good night's rest had never sounded so inviting.

As I lay awake that night in my crowded quarters, I began to think long and hard about my life. Once again, my mind flooded with regrets, the things I should have done and said, the moments I'd taken for granted, the people I'd hurt. I fully knew I could have been killed that day, and I was not in the right place with God. The idea of going to hell terrified me to no end, but I was still not ready to turn my heart over to God. It was safer to keep the walls up, push him away and pretend I didn't care. If he really wanted me back so badly, he could show up and tell me so himself.

In February 2006, our unit headed to Barrwanna. One rainy evening, I jumped in the back of a Humvee with another guy and headed down the bumpy road. We got only a mile outside the dam when the vehicle suddenly careened down a cliff. The next thing I knew, I was waking up underwater, panicked and gasping for air. It took me a few seconds to realize why everything was so black; I'd been crushed by the Humvee and had now become its hostage. If I didn't act quickly, the water would completely fill the vehicle and trap me for good!

The 115 pounds of gear on my back felt like a mountain of bricks as I tried to move forward. My body was weak, my mind was confused and I was running out of time. I had to muster what little strength I had left to escape. Frantically, I called out for my buddy.

"I'm okay, man!" he called back. "Let's get out of this thing!" To my relief, I saw one tiny spot that was open. With everything I had in me, I swam toward it and slipped out just in time.

At that moment, the last bit of adrenaline I'd used dried up, and my body gave out. Reaching up, I discovered my face was covered in blood from where the Humvee had crushed it. When help finally arrived, I was too weak to move. The medics transported me to the nearest hospital, where I learned I'd fractured my foot.

"It's a miracle you're even alive, son," the doctor told me gravely as he bandaged me up. "People who have Humvees roll over on them usually don't make it out. I'm amazed that your only major injury is a fractured foot. You must have some angels watching over you."

I should have been singing praises, but instead I was filled with anger. I'd prayed that God would show himself to me, yet even the very act of saving my life wasn't enough to break my walls down. Only later would I be able to look back and rejoice over his merciful hand on my life.

I spent the next month in the hospital recovering. During that time, I wrote letters to Trina, pouring out my heart and letting her know how much I missed her. Yet the only ones that arrived in return were from my family and her mother. My heart sank each time a new envelope showed up in my hands. More than ever, I was determined to win Trina's heart back.

LOST

I returned to the States and told my parents I didn't want them to come to my "Welcome Home" ceremony. I was still hobbling around on a broken foot, the memories of our deployment too fresh in my mind to be in good spirits. I tried to go on with normal life but found it difficult without all my military buddies surrounding me. They had become like brothers to me; I took immense comfort in knowing we were all treading the same waters. I felt like an alien back in the States, watching people go on with their lives like I hadn't been gone at all.

"So, how many people did you kill over there?" my old friends asked over and over again.

I shrugged and rolled my eyes. I wasn't really in the mood for this kind of conversation. As a young Marine, people seemed to view me as nothing more than a punk kid. They had no idea that I'd cheated death, driven Humvees and fired guns for the past few months. I began to grow depressed and started drinking again. The worse I felt, the more I drank. I continued to think about Trina, who still had yet to contact me. My heart ached for her, and until we could be together, I refused to date other women.

"What happened to you over there?" my buddy teased one day. "You turn gay or something? I saw that girl checkin' you out, and you didn't even glance her way."

I tried to ignore him. It wasn't the first time I'd been accused of being gay. I'd had girls throw themselves at me more than once, but I wasn't the least bit interested. The comments hurt but not as much as the hole in my heart. I liked women, but the problem was I only liked *one* woman. I could only hope and pray that someday Trina would forgive me and return her heart to me.

I tried praying again, mostly about Trina. I even fasted for a while, pleading with God to give her back. But when nothing happened, I grew even angrier. Where was this God who supposedly cared so much? If he was real, he would show up! Why wasn't he answering my prayers?!

When I wasn't drinking myself into a stupor, I tried talking more with my parents. Despite the walls I'd built between us, I'd missed them during my deployment. I knew deep down that they cared for me and wanted to be close again. I confided in my father, telling him how much I missed Trina and how scared I was that I'd lost her forever. He encouraged me to keep seeking God. I didn't have the heart to tell him that I'd nearly given up on God.

In April 2007, I returned to Iraq for the second time. On our ship ride over, our battalion commander pulled us together for a serious talk. "You guys are my main force on this deployment," he told us. "We're going to lose lives over here. I need you to give it your all. I see the leadership qualities in you. Now is the time to step it up and put them to use."

My heart beat with pride. I considered it an honor to defend my country. I would not let my people down!

We were set to clear the main supply routes and cities on a 20-mile highway just north of Fallujah when we arrived. Fallujah was the epicenter for terrorists from every nation. They had hung four Americans from the

LOST

bridge in the middle of the city; the house of hell was in this city. The house of hell was a previous mission; 13 Marines had gone in, and only four had survived. My new squad leader was in the house of hell and had almost lost his leg from an enemy grenade.

Just before we left the base to start the operation, I called my mom and told her we were going in. "I won't be able to contact you for a few weeks, so I just wanted to say … goodbye. For now." My throat caught as she began to cry. "I'll be okay; I promise," I added, trying to stay strong.

That night, I strapped 120 pounds of gear to my back and left for our mission. It was an unbearable 140 degrees outside, and within minutes of walking, I was miserable. We spent the next four weeks crawling around, clearing roads and houses and blowing up roadside bombs everywhere. I survived off of one meal a day; my only source of sustenance was water. At night, we sometimes slept in sewer ditches, the putrid smell irritating our nostrils as we tried to fall asleep. I had never been so uncomfortable or lonely in all my life.

One morning while watching for advancing platoons, I crawled up next to my buddy, Haynie, whose wife back home was expecting a child. Suddenly, rocks sprayed everywhere, and I realized we were being fired on. I jumped on Haynie and shouted at him to get down. After the fire ceased and I realized we were not being fired on, I turned to Haynie. "I promised your wife that I would bring you back, and I will do everything in my power to do that," I told him somberly.

WALLS

Glancing around, I began to panic. "Where's Gonzo?" I called out. Gonzo was one of my closest brothers. I raced down our defensive line checking for any casualties and placing Marines in better cover. I got to Gonzo's team, and Gonzo was not there. "Payvie, where's Gonzo?" He pointed to a body lying in the road. We had just walked up.

"Call in a bird. We have a man down!" I screamed as I ran to the scene.

Gonzo was already putting a life-saving tourniquet on his leg, and I immediately went to work on his chest and face, stopping the bleeding and covering it up. While Gonzo and I were moving around the body, I noticed there was another pressure plate four inches from Gonzo's foot. We stabilized him as he screamed in pain.

That night as I lay on the uncomfortable ground in my full body armor, I found it hard to sleep. I began to pray again, asking God to please show up in a real way. I was physically and emotionally spent, desperate to cling onto anything. I pulled out my iPod and began humming along to Christian songs. The words comforted my soul as they rang in my ears. I so wanted to find peace and happiness again, but was it too late?

A buddy across from me opened a letter from his girlfriend and got a big smile on his face. "Where's your fan mail, bro?" he asked, glancing over at me. "Not diggin' the ladies anymore?"

I glared at him. "Leave me alone, man." I was tired of taking the heat about being gay. How could I explain to

LOST

these guys that I just wanted one woman? I would wait forever for Trina if that's what it took.

One day, a letter with new handwriting came to me. It was from a girl named Jaimie; my mother had met her back in Alaska and suggested we start writing. Jaimie was a Christian and became a great encouragement to me. She wrote one letter after another, telling me to be strong, to keep trusting in the Lord and to rely on his faithfulness. Jaimie's letters were the highlight of my deployment and a welcome distraction from my thoughts about Trina. Slowly, my heart began to soften toward God.

In July, I lost two of my closest buddies. Stacy was killed by a sniper on July 5, and Stokes was killed on July 30 when he stepped on a landmine. Stokes had a wife and two children. I was wracked with grief and guilt. Why would God choose to take Stokes' life when he had a family back home? I had nothing going for me; why couldn't he have taken me instead? I missed my friends terribly, and once again, the reality of the danger we faced hit hard. I had reached a new low.

When we climbed back on the ship to head back to the States, I was physically and emotionally drained. Another letter showed up, this time from a guy named Al Phillips. He was a friend of the family back in Alaska. "I hope to encourage you," he wrote. "I sense that you are worn out and at the end of your rope. I had a vision of you being physically fit once again, your strength restored. I pray you hold on and trust in God, for he will carry you through this difficult time." His words spoke volumes to my soul. Instantly, I felt refreshed, as though someone had poured a cool drink down my throat and washed away my thirst. I cried for an hour straight that night.

By the time we reached Camp Pendleton and got off the ship, I'd gotten into a fistfight and bloodied my lip and face. I was less than thrilled about being back in California. Jaimie and I began talking on the phone. I was always encouraged by our conversations. She was a comfort to me during one of the darkest times of my life. I expressed feeling unsettled and out of place back in the States. I was still grieving my two friends and needed time to heal. Jaimie was patient and kind, just the sort of friend I needed. I had no idea where our relationship was headed, but for now, I enjoyed her company.

I began speaking with my parents and was finally able to open up to them a bit. I felt the walls inside my heart start to come down, but I kept my guard up, unwilling to let them see I was changing. There were too many years of hurt on the line; I had to play it cool.

I'd looked all over for a specific Nissan Xterra SUV. When I found one on eBay and discovered it was located in New Jersey, I decided to make the trip. On my way back, I stopped and saw Jaimie in Pennsylvania. I was attracted to her in person, and we went on a few dates while I was in town. I enjoyed her company immensely, but my heart still belonged to Trina.

Not long after I returned to California, I heard the Marines were taking volunteers for another deployment to Fallujah. I eagerly signed up to go. "This is your last chance," I told God. "You better show up in a big way, and if you don't, I don't want to return from this deployment." I was still fighting depression, despite having made baby steps with my relationships and my faith. Often, I thought that maybe being dead would be easier than living life. As I boarded the ship, I glanced back at the crystal Pacific, wondering if I'd ever see it again.

Fallujah had stabilized quite a bit since we'd last been there. We drove through the city, observing bullet-ridden buildings, recalling the horror that had ensued the years before. We escorted VIPs and other important government officials around, thankful to not be in the line of fire this time. But when a car bomb went off one day near our convoy, the images came flooding back. As we were forced to pick body parts up off the road, I felt myself grow nauseous. I pictured Stacy and Stokes, so brave, unaware that their lives were about to come to an end that fateful day. I tried to be strong, but inside I felt myself grow weaker.

After returning to the States, I began work as a lifeguard to finish up my last two months in the Marines and started attending Saddleback Church. Jaimie and I were still in contact, and she'd sent me the book *The Purpose Driven Life* by Rick Warren, pastor of Saddleback. I was highly encouraged by the book, which challenges us all to embrace the purpose to which God has called us. I'd thought my sole purpose in life was to defend my country, but my experiences overseas had only left me traumatized and depressed. I sensed that God wanted more from me, but I had no idea how to move on.

I began seeing a therapist in hopes that I could sort out my feelings. During the first few sessions, I poured out my heart to the woman, sobbing in her office until I was drained. I expected to receive amazing revelations that would help me begin functioning again, but I only left feeling more defeated.

My parents had moved back to Alaska and were still in contact with Trina's family. One day an old youth pastor's wife, Jessie Roberson, called with an invitation I couldn't pass up. "We're all going to John's Island with your family and Trina's family," she told me. "You should come, Daniel. It will be so good for you to get away. And you could see Trina again."

I was elated. I pictured myself hand-in-hand with Trina, walking along the water, laughing and talking like we had in the good old days. Surely, things would be the same when we reunited! I packed my bags and counted the days until we departed.

To my disappointment, Trina was distant when we met up. I tried my best to talk with her, but everything felt strained.

"Can we just start over as friends?" I asked Trina as we strolled along the water one night, the moon winking in the distance. We had barely spoken in the last couple of years. Trina looked just as beautiful as ever, and I so badly wanted to take her in my arms and make everything go back to the way it was, but I knew we were a long way from that.

LOST

"I just need time, Daniel," Trina sighed. "You've been gone a long time. And a lot has happened to both of us."

You have no idea, I wanted to tell her. *You have no idea.*

While on the island, I experienced a terrible nightmare. In it, I was back in Iraq watching people be killed, blood spattering everywhere. The images were very vivid and disturbing, and I woke up in a sweat. The nightmare would be the first of many more to come.

With my Marine duties coming to an end, I began packing my gear and counting the days until I could move home and start a new life. I returned to Alaska and began attending church. Week after week, I sat in the pew on Sunday morning crying until I could not get another tear out. I felt so alone, exhausted and misunderstood. At home, the nightmares continued, and I grew depressed. I cried out to God, but my prayers seemed to vanish into an empty vacuum.

At last, I mustered the courage to go forward for prayer one Sunday morning. My brother and his wife stood at the front of the church as I made my way forward, my legs shaking so terribly I feared they might give way.

"I ... can't ..." I began, sobbing uncontrollably. I could not finish my sentence. They laid a gentle hand on my shoulder as I continued to cry. The pain was all too fresh, the memories too vivid. When would it stop?

One day, my nephew dropped a toy on the ground just outside my room. I had just laid down to sleep, but the jingling noise jarred me so badly that I nearly jumped off the bed. Even the smallest things frightened me these days: a slamming door, loud footsteps, the faucet turning on. I could not sit down with a window behind me. My edginess only made me more depressed.

One Sunday, my mother suggested I go forward and talk with Gretchen Humphrey, a member of the prayer team. Gretchen was known to have amazing words from God. I'd given up on counseling and had very little hope left; what could it hurt to go talk to the woman?

Slowly, I strode to the front of the church, my heart pounding under the dim lights. Gretchen was standing just a few feet away, an inviting smile on her face. I didn't plan to pour my guts out to her, but before I knew it, I found myself sharing about Stokes and Stacy, my two buddies I'd lost overseas. "I feel so worthless and guilty to be alive when my friends are not," I cried. "I feel like there is this dark force surrounding me, trying to destroy me."

Gretchen put a gentle hand on my shoulder and said these words: "Can you put a label on that dark force?"

I paused and wiped away the tears. "Worthlessness and guilt," I whispered at last. "And regret."

Gretchen nodded. "Okay." She prayed over me, asking God to relieve me of these feelings. I repeated the words after her through my tears. When we both opened our eyes, I felt a renewed sense of hope, a peace I hadn't felt in years.

"Thank you," I choked out. "You don't know how much that meant."

My parents had opened a new church in Alaska. A

man on the prayer team, whose name was Kendell Meek, approached me one day with another word from God. "God showed me that you have scales on your heart, that you need to let him in so that he can remove those scales," he told me.

I nodded, for I knew he was right. Scales, walls, call them what you want, but he was right. I'd spent half my life keeping up walls, trying to protect my heart from more hurt, running from God to avoid accepting his unconditional love. It was time to peel off those scales and break down those walls once and for all. I cried out to God, asking him to do just that. "Lord, I'm sorry for running. I'm sorry for not believing you. I choose to believe that you have a purpose for my life, that you do love me. Please help me to trust you."

I cried my way through church for a year straight. Ever so slowly, though, I felt my heart begin to heal. The nightmares slowly subsided, and for the first time in years, I had motivation to wake up in the morning. I felt like a baby learning to take his first steps; it required putting one foot in front of the other each day, trusting that God would guide the way. The healing would take time, but I was hopeful that my heart would be restored completely someday.

In 2009, my friend Alex Johnson and his brother came out from Missouri to visit. When my father offered to baptize us, I was excited. We were slowly making headway in our relationship, and I wanted to give him that opportunity to be a part of such a special event.

WALLS

"I baptize you in the name of the Father, the Son and the Holy Spirit!" my father announced as I rose from the water. A part of me felt truly alive again; what a wonderful feeling to know I'd been redeemed! I was starting to feel excited about my faith again and wanted to share it with others.

Jaimie moved to Alaska for an internship, and we began dating more seriously. She bought me a book called *Way of the Wild Heart* by John Eldridge. The book depicted a man's heart in a way I'd never thought about before. As I turned the pages, I realized how much anger I'd stored up toward my father for his years of neglect. I was finally able to see that my father had done the best he could, that he had always loved me, even when he had not said it aloud. I called my dad shortly after with these simple words, "I love you, Dad." It was the first time I'd been able to say that to him in 10 years, and we both cried.

I bought my first house in 2010 and began getting excited about the idea of setting down in Alaska. The fragments of my heart were starting to piece together, and I found myself living life again. When summer ended and Jaimie's internship wrapped up, I knew in my heart that our relationship had run its course. Jaimie did not want to stay in Alaska, and I now called it my home. I cared for Jaimie, and she had been a huge encouragement in my life, but my heart told me God had other plans. Deep down, I still longed for Trina.

In August 2010, I was working on an oil rig, dismantling a large 500-pound pipe, when it swung back and fell on my leg. Instantly, pain seared me as blood trickled out of the wound. I squeezed the wound as tight as I could while I called for help.

Five minutes passed before help came, but it felt like five hours. The pipe had come within 4 millimeters of my artery; I could have easily bled to death if it had been punctured. As the paramedics life-lifted me to the hospital, I lay back on the stretcher and began to pray. The old Daniel would have gotten angry and thrown out one cuss word after another, but I clenched my teeth despite the pain and tried to pray. This was a true sign God was working on my heart!

"You were the most pleasant patient I've ever had," the doctor told me with a grin.

Unable to get off the couch for a couple of weeks, I holed up in my house, trying to find ways to pass the time while my leg healed. One day, a surprise visitor showed up at my door. It was Trina! She looked more beautiful than ever and was truly a sight for sore eyes. "Wow, nice to see you!" I cried.

"Heard you might need a nurse," she said with a wry smile. "Mind if I sit down?"

I smiled back. "Be my guest. I'm not going anywhere."

Trina and I had lots to catch up on. We swapped one story after another, laughing and sharing our hearts. I was so thankful we'd reunited, yet my heart was still cautious. This was the only girl I'd ever loved, the one I had waited for. Was it possible God had brought her back into my life for good this time?

WALLS

One night as I sat talking with my mother, she shared something important with me. "I never told you this, Daniel, but there was this time a few years ago when you were deployed. I had this vision that you were being attacked. Suddenly, an angel was standing behind you with huge body armor and a sword, protecting you."

I got goose bumps as she relayed the exact day and time her vision had occurred. I had been in peril that night, but thanks to my angel, who I later named Taj, God had protected me. All those years, I'd been crying out to God, asking him for bigger and better signs, when all along he'd been right there saying, "Don't you see, Daniel? Don't you see I have never forsaken you?"

Since my accident, I've spent a lot of time staring at my four walls. Thanks to Trina, my new girlfriend, I've been a bit distracted. But it's gotten me thinking about those walls again, the ones I put up in my heart for so long. I swore I'd never let them come down. But even a Marine can't always be tough. I thank God that he broke down the walls and helped me slowly rebuild. My heart is healing again, thanks to the one in charge. My assignment is clear: Share the good news of Christ and the hope he's given me. And my deployment starts now.

CONCLUSION

Stranded, isolated, alone and hopeless …

It was early March, and I was lost in the Alaskan wilderness. I had made several wrong decisions, numerous wrong turns and was simply in the wrong place at the wrong time. Fifteen degrees and soaking wet, I was in trouble!

I'll never forget the soft yet distinct sound in the night as I slipped in and out of consciousness. It was a murmur at first, then a hum and finally the full-blown cacophony of a U.S. Coast Guard MH-60 Jayhawk helicopter. I can't possibly express the relief I felt at that moment. I was overcome by an awareness that I was not alone, that I had not been forgotten, that someone was aware of my situation and cared about my rescue. It wasn't the sound of the chopper that I heard in that moment, it was the sound of HOPE!

I want you to know that this is exactly what my desire is for you as you read the stories compiled in these few pages. I want you to hear the faint hum of HOPE coming into your situation, and I pray you discover that rescue is possible for all who have lost their way.

I will never forget the moment I discovered that rescue was available for me, even though I had *"made several wrong decisions, numerous wrong turns and was simply in the wrong place at the wrong time"* far more often than

LOST

I would like to admit in my life. The discovery that someone had come for my rescue has forever changed my life.

Growing up, I believed that there was some magical prayer, some "silver bullet" that would get me a ticket on the train to heaven. I believed that if I said the right words or prayed with the right person, then God would be willing to accept my plea and grant me a seat on the "Glory Train."

What I have discovered over the past 22 years, though, is that God is only after one thing — my affection. He wants our hearts. Our humble and hungry heart crying out for the rescue we find in Jesus *is* the singular thing God desires and requires.

For me, it sounded something like this:

God, I need you! Nothing I have tried has even come close to producing what it promised, and I want to give myself to you. I'm humbled that you would accept me, and I'm forever grateful for the price Jesus paid for my rescue. Forgive me, heal me, hold me, Father. In the name of Jesus I ask it, amen.

I really couldn't possibly describe the *"cacophony"* of emotion, elation and enjoyment I felt in that moment. The realization *"that I was not alone, that I had not been forgotten, that someone was aware of my situation and cared about my rescue"* was simply overwhelming.

So my prayer for you is that you may discover, like so many others have before you, that you are not alone, that you have not been forgotten, that someone is aware of

CONCLUSION

your situation and cares about your rescue and that Jesus is not simply our hope, but he desires to be our salvation!

Grace and Peace to You,
Pastor Jonathan Walker

We would love for you to join us at our Wasilla, Palmer or North (Talkeetna) Campus!

Please call us at 907.373.7910 for directions, or contact us at www.churchontherockak.org.

Wasilla Campus

We meet Sundays at
3571 Machen Road, Wasilla, AK 99687
(Mile 45.5 on the Parks Hwy)

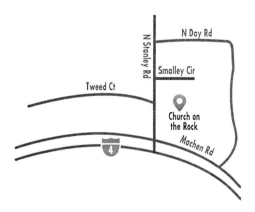

Palmer Campus

We meet Sundays at
619 E Scott Road, Palmer, AK 99645

North (Talkeetna) Campus

We meet Sundays at
16246 E. Sunshine Drive, Talkeetna, AK 99676
(Mile 99 on the Parks Hwy)

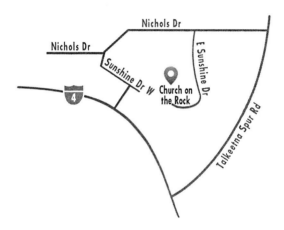